On a Lighter Note

Melodie Corrigall

ISBN: 978-93-88319-32-4

First Edition: 2020
Rs. 200/-

Cyberwit.net
HIG 45 Kaushambi Kunj, Kalindipuram
Allahabad - 211011 (U.P.) India
http://www.cyberwit.net
Tel: +(91) 9415091004
E-mail: info@cyberwit.net

Printed at Thomson Press India Limited.

Contents

Polar Bear Perils

July 25th, a Tuesday, Tessa greeted the day with a certain confidence that a polar bear would not attack her. On reflection, she wondered if she was being overly optimistic. In life, nothing was certain.

With global warming, the polar bear's traditional food supply was rapidly diminishing. Like her, bears got hungry. She couldn't live on hope and they couldn't live on snow. If famished, a polar bear might eat a human, should one be on offer. A few months earlier, a polar bear had attacked campers in Norway or some such place.

As she prepared for the day, Tessa rolled the word "certain" around in her mouth. The word felt as round and cool as an ice pellet. Tessa had always found shelter from the unpredictable storms of life within the cozy igloo created by words. Correctly applied, their sharp edges, and reliable colours appealed.

Although not colourful, white was her favourite for its uncompromising stance. To gaze at the horizon and see a smooth flat surface—white from the night's snowfall—gave one a settled feeling, unless a polar bear was heading in your direction.

Certainty, except in words, was illusive. So much of what Tessa had been told as a child, drilled into her as a student, smeared with as a TV viewer, turned out to be fake. Raised on a diet of white bread and roses, her adult life was bullied by thorns and multigrain buns. Still she tried to face each day with a realistic appraisal of perils, ready to face whatever the tempest blew her way.

Living just off Yonge Street in downtown Toronto, the largest city in Canada, she trusted that her confidence in relation to avoiding a polar bear attack that day was not just wishful thinking.

(Originally published: *Switchback Flash Contest*, 2011)

The Red Car

Stanley was struggling to get the front door key out of the lock, a sagging bag of groceries on his hip, when his wife Moira, sporting her designer sunglasses, confronted him. Her steely accusation, "I saw your car today" stopped him in his tracks.

"You were in Burnaby?" he asked clutching his drooping bag of groceries.

"No, in Kerrisdale on 41st."

"My car and I were in Burnaby."

"That's where I thought you were going."

"And right you were."

"If I'd known you were coming into Vancouver, I'd have met you for lunch."

"As always."

"Your car was smack in front of my favourite Italian restaurant."

"Where we'd have met."

"With a scarf in the back seat."

"*Your* scarf?"

"Not my scarf, an expensive pink scarf."

"Then you knew."

"I thought you'd taken my advice about your secretary."

"To buy her a scarf?"

"No, Dumbo, to thank her for her extra work."

"She's well paid."

"I didn't expect you to take her to lunch at my favourite restaurant."

"It wasn't my car," her husband sighed, pulling wilted leeks from the grocery bag.

"But then," his wife said, voice rising. "I checked the front seat and spied the satellite radio."

"Which, thanks to you, I don't have."

"Why should you hear news from Japan if I can't afford a spa weekend?"

"It's the BBC news I listen to."

"Wherever. So there it was, bold as brass."

"Check my car. There's no satellite radio in my car."

"Easy enough to hide."

"For God's sakes, Moira, get real."

"I was beginning to steam. Last Tuesday when you said you were having a drink with the guys you were probably with scarf lady."

"Where is this going?" Stanley said, grabbing a cloth to sop up the melting ice cream.

Moira grabbed the soggy carton, yanked open the freezer and chucked it in, then turned to her husband, and leaned forward, her shoulders as high as a hawk's.

"By now, I was furious: no lunch, sugar level soaring."

"Then you checked the license plates and saw the car wasn't mine."

"I don't know your plate number but I know your red car. You'd left the window open—an expensive radio and you leave the window open."

"Which I never do since they stole our hamster."

"The fight was on," his wife cried, eyes gleaming. "I leaned into the car, grabbed the scarf and hurled it into a puddle. Then I dove in, snatched the radio wires and yanked them out. I felt vindicated—like a warrior goddess. There I stood righteously, wires hanging from my hand like dead snakes, when I heard a god awful screech. A mad man was hurtling towards me."

"'What the fuck are you doing?'" he yelled, without even a 'Pardon my French.'"

"Bloody busybody, I thought and whipped around to see a loony man, hair sticking up as if he'd been hit by lightening heading for me like a linebacker. I snarled right back. 'Fuck off. It's my business what I do to my husband's car.'"

"'It's *my* car you old bag and that's *my* radio,' he screeched."

"His eyes were rolling and his arms flailing. I put up my dukes."

"You hit him?" Stanley groaned.

Moira whipped off her glasses to display her purple eye. "He hit me back. You should have been there to defend me."

"For god's sakes, Moira, I was in Burnaby."

"'You bugger,' I shouted back. 'I'm old enough to be your mother and you hit me,'"

"What next?" Stanley squeaked.

"Some bloody do-gooder called the police. It was chaos: crazy with people coming out of the woodwork to join the fray."

"What did they do?" her husband whispered.

"I told the policeman it was an honest mistake but the cop sided with the crazy guy."

"But they let you go?"

"Sure, but you have to come to the station with me tomorrow."

"Me? Why me?"

"To explain about the car."

(Originally published: SpeKulative Stories Anthology, 2016)

Slicker-Down

When the Bellybob town council announced the Most Outrageous Cat contest Tania's friends knew that Slicker-Down was a shoe-in for the $1,000 prize. Tania, however, was adamant that her cat would not compete.

"I don't want Slicker-Down exploited," she said. "If his antics are on the Internet he might get kidnapped." Her friend Dolly erupted with laughter, "Good luck for you. If he's kidnapped, refuse to pay and they'll be stuck with him."

The contest was a first for Bellybob and was intended to put the town on the map. Three years earlier, Lillyworth, five miles down the highway, had hosted a competition for the most adventurous dog, and followed up with a dog show at the country fair. Local businesses hooked their wagons to the marketing ploy. Now Lillyworth had annual Dog Days and been shortlisted as Dog Town, an annual honor sponsored by Doggie Yummies, two years running.

Always one to look for the main chance, Bellybob's mayor wanted to do something equally successful. "A contest for prettiest cat would be boring," he insisted and challenged the council to come up with a more creative idea. The suggestion by gun totting Whig Wanderbee to have a Cat With the Most Kills contest didn't fly because Councilor Betsy Witherspoon abhorred the idea of "profiting from murder." Finally, the thinking-outside-the- box-communication guru convinced the council to focus the prize on the most rascally cat.

Those who knew Slicker-Down's reputation assumed there could be no contest. He ran his owner's life to shreds. When anyone dropped by, he had to be incarcerated in the basement, which had been soundproofed on his behalf. When Tania's friends or relatives from out of town visited, she was forced to put S-D, as she called him, at a cat retreat for the weekend.

"Who knows what he might do?" Tania wailed. "He'd pounce at you from the stairs. Leap on the table and lap up your tea. He'd snatch the soother out of a baby's mouth."

Slicker-Down was particularly naughty when Tania was on the phone. "Just like my daughter," Dolly said. "She'll play quietly when I am working in the kitchen but the minute I'm on the phone, she'll bellow. If I take her up, she screams into the receiver. They seem to know."

Slicker-Down sure knew and he had a short fuse. Five minutes into any phone call just when Dolly, Maria or another friend were explaining in detail the operation they had for varicose veins, or a sales item they'd returned twice, Slicker-Down started up.

"Oh my god," Tania would cry. "He's climbing up the curtains. I've got to go."

"My orchid," she'd shout. "He's eating the flowers. Talk to you soon."

Tania never had to say who "he" was. She lived alone, except for Slicker-Down: any damages were his.

Most cats mellow with age, Slicker-Down lived well past the expected date for cats and only got wilder. (A friend had suggested she should enter him in the Guinness Book of Records for long life.)

When Tania stayed firm on her contest decision, her friends, acknowledging that she was as stubborn as her cat, stopped pestering her.

All went well until three days before the contest deadline when Lucille, an old acquaintance, hoping to find a career-launching story, appeared at Tania's door.

"Surprise," the journalist cried, herself surprised at the horrified face that greeted her. "I'm in town doing a feature on the Contest and I want to write about the notorious Slicker-Down." Pointing to her photographer colleague, she pushed forward. "We're ready to roll."

"Sorry," Tania cried, clutching her mouth and holding off the marauders. "I had something for lunch that won't stay down," she cried as she slammed the door shut. Her friend Lucille called through the mail slot, "Drink some water and baking soda. I'll be back at six."

Tania hurried out the back door and headed down the alley determined to find a cat sniffing around a garbage can or skulking in someone's garden. She spotted a ragged old scoundrel, scooped him up, squeezed his squawking figure close and ran home. Shoving the struggling feline in the hall cupboard, Tania hurried out to the cat store. Once there, she scooped up a few cans of high-end cat food and a supply of catnip. (A friend had told her that catnip drove cats wild.) Once safely home, Tania sprinkled catnip around the house.

When she opened the cupboard door, the cat shot out, leapt in the air, its hair as if on fire, twirled around in frenzy and slid across the floor.

"Good boy," said Tania.

The trial demonstration was not a moment too soon. The local paparazzi were at the door. Tania headed for the hallway, ready to face the world. She welcomed the twosome into the kitchen and pointed to the cat, which after its frenzied spin around the house, leapt unto the kitchen table and licked the butter dish. "I apologize that he looks so ratty," Tania said to her visitors. "He fights like hell if I try to wash him."

"Typical scoundrel," said the photographer, an admirer of feisty cats and women.

Stretched like a lion errant on the kitchen table, the afternoon sun golden against his shabby coat, the cat's purr stopped them cold.

"I knew it," cried the reporter.

"Knew what?" Tania asked.

"I hate cats but they love me. No way could I get one to act up."

"It's not that," said the photographer.

"No, I'm sure she's right," Tania said.

"No. Cats are clever. You want him to be a scoundrel and so he's acting like a lamb."

Tania sighed. "I wish I'd known that."

The three of them rolled their eyes and laughed indulgently. No way would wily Slicker-Down oblige by winning a bad cat contest.

Slicker-Down rose, head high, tail swishing and sauntered from the room. His first meal of the morning had been a scrawny mouse but now his future was assured.

(Originally published: *Contrary Cats*, 2012)

Table Man

Gillian wasn't a practicing Christian but she thought Jesus, had things been different, would have made a loving husband. Always a good sign when a man is close to his mom and Jesus' mother wasn't the only Mary who thought he was great. So when she saw the personal ad, Gillian was captivated.

"I can't walk on water," it read, "But I'm up to the mark in other ways. My calling starts with a C." *Table Man*

Obviously it was from a carpenter who wasn't pretending to be Jesus but did aspire along the God is Love line: a sort of latter day hippie carpenter. Table Man obviously specialized in tables but what kind: modern or rustic? It set Gillian to wondering what type of furniture Jesus had built.

Gillian immediately responded to the ad and as quick as fast sealing glue, she and Table Man, happily from the same town, had set up a meeting at a local café. They arrived within minutes of each other and settled at a corner table. After a discussion about bus schedules, he blurted, "I bet you're an Au woman not an Ag woman. "

Astonished by his opener Gillian replied with her planned witticism, "Here you are Table Man at a table."

"Speaking of tables," he replied, "my favorite is the Periodic. Is it yours?"

Taken aback by the turn of events, Gillian grasped for a response. Risking a rift so early in the relationship she opted for honesty, "No, I prefer constants—like the Times Table."

(Originally published: Caffeine Presse, 2013)

The Dominant Duo

She was at the gate but entrance, to Tilley's surprise, was not automatic. The woman ahead of her in line, tousled and troubled, was being held up as the gatekeeper rustled through his cards for her credentials. Cards! The organization was behind the times and, naturally, an eye scan was not possible.

Tilley had assumed they would have a record of who she was. She expected them to be like Santa and know if she were good or bad. Hopefully, they wouldn't be petty enough to worry about a lapsed membership.

Off to her left, an alternate door of bristly steel caught Tilley's eye. A well-endowed woman in a svelte red dress beckoned her over. When Tilley shook her head, a slender young man replaced the woman. Ignoring his inviting smile, she swung around to discover the person ahead still agitating for entry. It was worse than trying to get past a bicep-rich bouncer.

Her father had always insisted it was all in whom you knew, he being comfortably ensconced with the influential. He was right, had she been a more steadfast member she might have been whisked through the line. Unfortunately she had been an independent thinker.

In recent years, when she started getting creaky bones, she had been courted with pleas to join up: declare her affiliation. She should have responded to the opposing sides' propaganda and chosen one or the other.

A skeptic, reluctant to jump on board with causes or clubs, Tilley had dismissed the extreme alternatives. Both sides insisted that only they offered a sane solution. One offered short, the other long term, benefits. If you cast your ballot for one, you might suffer now, but if you chose the other you would suffer later. So whether to be hurled forward in a hand basket to hell, as one leader insisted would happen if she didn't come on board with him, or to be floated into the heavens for an idyllic life as the opposition insisted was on offer if she opted for her. Dismissing both sides as junk mail, she had dallied, hoping for a third choice—an independent party—for those not ready to sign up for either one of the dominant duo.

"No vote is a vote for the winning party," a friend had insisted. "Once the polls are closed and you sigh the last breath, too late to change your mind."

So here she was, no way to slip through the gateway but finally her turn at the gate. The frail custodian in his beige jacket leaned forward—were those wings on his back? —"Ready to join the throng," he invited. Still she hesitated.

To her side the woman in red, skirt slit to the thigh, reappeared. "Still time to choose us," she crooned. "With global warming, you're used to hot weather. And we offer more fun than you'd have playing a harp."

"We've changed with the times," the winged gate man barked. "We have electric keyboards."

"Whatever," said the lady in red, dismissively?

(Originally published: *Corner Bar Magazine*, 2017)

Phoenix Rises

Tomorrow would be the "new start day" Kevin promised himself. But how to start?

The mid-term essay was due at 9 the next morning; as yet his efforts were a clutter of disjointed paragraphs and midnight false starts. Drifting along, brushing past other straggling students, Kevin kicked at the papers tumbling across the campus quad and twisted absentmindedly at his loose jacket button.

He should get back to the library and buckle down. More urgently, he ought to phone Jerry to beg a few bucks to pay the rent. But his cell phone needed recharging and he didn't know where the nearest pay phone was.

The campus lights (recently installed and touted as environmentally friendly) were dim and the persistent drizzle made the air heavy. When the button popped off in his hand, Kevin pushed it into his jacket pocket. If he could find some thread, any colour, he'd sew it back on. Another two buttons awaited a similar fate.

Although it was early September, stress and lack of sleep chilled him to the bone. A heavier jacket would have been in order. He'd forgotten his winter one at his old apartment; next time he saw Arnie, he'd ask him to bring it to class.

First things first: the essay was due tomorrow. Who could he coax to help him at this late date? Sheila had written most of his first one but now she was hanging out with Geoff, so it wasn't likely she'd bother to give him a hand.

Kevin had promised himself he'd be more "proactive" (Sheila's term) but couldn't think how to do that. Suddenly he was jolted alert by the sound of a chorus of moans. It reminded him of the print of mangled images of souls suffering in hell that had hung in his Sunday school classroom. Many a nightmare had been invoked by those faded images, although no change in behavior.

The groans came from an open basement door. Without warning, as if awakened by the human grumbling, the sky spit out a torrent of chilling rain. Kevin clutched his papers to his chest; he hadn't been able to find his knapsack that morning.

Curious about the sound and desperate to avoid the wet onslaught, he slipped through the open door. He blinked to see what looked like an inferno on a bare stage. It was an old theatre, with rows of empty stalls. Shaking his damp jacket, Kevin slipped into an aisle seat and stared at the mass of bodies contorting and writhing in a fleshy mass on stage. No escape for them either, he thought. Then like a colourful phoenix, a flame rose. It was a girl, thin as a knife, her arms stretched above her head. The mass lifted her up. A cry, like a burst of sex, split from her lips.

Although she was covered in a body suit, Kevin recognized his dream girl immediately. She was the latecomer in his English class. Every week she burst into the room ten minutes into the lecture, just as he was dozing off, with a different exotic hair color. The strands jutted up in all directions as if she had been struck by lightening. Her clothes were bizarre. Who knew where she found them. Multi-colored jackets like Joseph of Arimathea's, sequined jump suits like Elvis Presley, capes like Superman.

Kevin seldom remembered what the professor said but he never forgot how his muse looked. His daydream was startled awake by a harsh male voice, "Can I help you?" Kevin looked behind alarmed alert by the huge looming figure.

"Come to volunteer? Good. Jim said you might be by."

Before he could sputter a protest, Kevin was lifted from his seat and dragged toward the stage.

"So what will it be? Painting? We expect to be here all night."

"Actually," Kevin began, recalling the paint streaks on his parent's bathroom from his efforts and his essay due the next morning.

"Stop," a voice called from the balcony, the moving mass on stage froze.

"Good, they're taking a break," his guide said. "You can say hello to the cast before you set to work."

Laughing and pushing against one another the actors moved to the front of the stage to welcome the volunteer. "The man who'll save our bacon," someone cried.

And there she was, aglow, "Well, it's my English guy," his phoenix said. "Do a good job and quickly. I don't want to have my bum streaked with wet paint."

Kevin visualized her bare bottom in Technicolor—pink, plump and painted. She swooped down and gave him a wet peck, freezing him on the spot. He tried to explain the essay (and didn't she too have an essay due?) but something had happened to his voice.

His guide laughed as the girl turned away. "Actors," he said, "so dramatic. Lucky we're more down to earth and get things done. Tom, by the way, and I forgot your name."

"Kevin Campbell."

"Forget last names. No one will remember."

"What's the girl's name?" he asked.

"Becky, but not Becky Sharp, Becky Nightly."

Kevin suspected, as an English major, he should recognize the Sharp reference but his mind was blank.

Before he could object, Kevin was in a white paper overall, paint brush in hand, slapping on primer. All around others were laughing, protesting and pushing against one another. Hours passed, Kevin's arm ached, whenever he thought they might be done, someone brought in something more to paint. It was three o'clock before Tom announced it was time to go home.

"The janitor is having a fit. I'll slap the last bit on tomorrow morning."

As he was leaving, Kevin's Phoenix popped her heard around the corner. "If you come to opening night, you're invited to the cast party," she called and then vanished.

Suddenly alone, Kevin struggled in the dim light to find his way out of the building.

Wending his way back to his room, Kevin realized he didn't have details about the opening, which presumably was the next night. Was it in that basement theatre or somewhere else and at what time? He'd check it out the next day at English class. Now he had an excuse to talk to her—theatre buddies that they were.

The following morning scrambling for an excuse for the late essay, Kevin made it into class and settled down beside his friend Rodger.

"You won't believe what happened to me last night?"

"You finished your essay?"

"No, I met up with that beautiful girl in our class?"

"What beautiful girl?"

"The one at the back who's always late?"

His friends swung around to check. "What girl?"

"She's not here yet. We were up all night?"

"You slept with her?"

"No, I was painting."

His friend looked back. "I don't know who you mean. There's only that ghostly girl who wears the brown cape."

The professor droned on but Kevin hardly heard a word. By lecture's end his neck ached from swinging back and forth and still no Phoenix. Of course, it was crazy, to expect her. The cast was probably doing a final rehearsal before the show opened that night. Why else would they have worked so late the previous evening?

On the professor's final word, Kevin burst out of the classroom ignoring the dire warning about late essays. This was more important. He was needed elsewhere.

In the harsh sunlight, it took Kevin a few minutes to locate the alley he'd gone down the night before; everything looked differently in the day. Finally he noticed the tipped garbage can. This was it. He ducked around the corner, rushed to the side of the building and stopped short. Where the night before the theatre door had been, there was an enormous hole. At the bottom an orange excavator was struggling to dig deeper.

(Originally published: *Bethlehem Writers Roundtable*, 2013)

Mendelssohn's Eye

Since waking that Sunday, April had been in a tizzy, anxious to reveal her creativity to her husband Fred. She'd have happily snapped the laggard from his snores but, finding the bed empty, had hurried to the kitchen. To her disappointment, she'd discovered it was deserted. Her suspicions that Fred had ducked down to the garage to "check out the new guy" were later confirmed.

Having nailed down her inspirational words on a notepad, ready on the bedside table, as advised by a writer's magazine, April awaited Fred's return, flitting impatiently from feeding chickens to doing laundry to vacuuming the upstairs hall.

The moment she heard the front door open, she grabbed her masterpiece, and rushed downstairs to corner her husband. As quick as she had been, Fred was already crunched into his kitchen chair and was sipping coffee out of his Best Dad cup. The inspired poet cleared her throat, and proudly recited her verse.

Red berry Ruth

Blueberry Pie

They all had enough

For Mendelssohns eye.

After the final phrase settled into the room, only the sound of a persistent wasp, caught behind the ill-fitting screen, cut through the dead-sea silence.

April waited anxiously, aware that it would take her husband—who was no poet—time to digest the verse. But when, instead of words of wonder, a stilted heaviness descended, she despaired.

Always slow on the draw when replying to his wife, this time Fred had been stunned into silence. He scratched his cheeks rough from his early morning shave and swished his coffee around. "Wasn't Mendelssohn the guy who said two peas aren't alike?" he asked tentatively.

"No, dough boy" April snapped, "He's a composer."

When she scribbled down the poem, she recognized that Mendelssohn was famous but for what she wasn't sure. She'd checked on line to discover that Mendelssohn, long dead, was a celebrated musician. Although she often listened to music when she was feeding the cows, she couldn't remember any of Mendelssohn's tunes.

"Would I know any of his jingles?" her husband had asked suspiciously.

"No, but it's music poetry people know."

"You're sure you got the words right?"

"Of course, I wrote it down as soon as I got up," she said, handing him the paper.

Fred tugged his glasses out of his shirt pocket, cautioning April not to nag about the two broken pairs he'd similarly stored. Peering hopefully through the grimy lenses, he slowly picked over the lines.

Red berry Ruth

Blueberry Pie

They all had enough

For Mendelssohns eye.

"Shouldn't it be Mendelssohn's eye with a possessive mark?" he finally asked.

Didn't that sum him up, April thought. Where she discovered poetry, Fred was caged in a world of punctuation marks.

"Never mind," she'd snapped, snatching the paper from him and sailing out of the room.

Fortunately, for all concerned, the crack of the screen door slamming shut muffled Fred's query about lunch.

April headed across the field on a brisk walk to let off steam. Was she expecting too much of Fred? After all, everyone couldn't be a poet nor could everyone appreciate poetry. Fred did contribute to her art by driving her into town in stormy weather to attend her writing group. She wondered if Mendelssohn had had a wife and if so whether she had been supportive of his efforts.

Finally, her legs starting to tire, April decided it was best to go home and call a truce. As always, it was she who had suffered but, from all she had read on the subject, that's what made artists great: suffering.

She'd make some waffles. That should bring Fred back to the house. And she'd not even comment when he drowned them in Maple Syrup. She'd even join him—even though she was trying to cut down on her carbs. After all, it has been a hard day, and even poets had to eat.

(Originally published: *Secrets and Dreams Anthology*, 2016)

Rosebud

Shivering in the cold night air, my arthritic fingers reluctant participants in my struggle I scrounged in my purse desperate to find the scrap of paper with the hotel address that had eluded me on my first ten searches. If I didn't find it and soon I'd be sleeping beside some homeless guy in a back alley. Nothing on earth would persuade me to do an ET and phone home.

What a sucker I am. I'd sold myself on this outing as a fun adventure. A chance to show my family there was life in the old dame yet. And that's how I had envisioned it, curled up in my twin bed at home under the ratty old horse blanket covering my daughter-in-law's satin quilt. The blanket is a necessary eyesore as it protects me from the cool house temperature my son insists on as his contribution to a green world.

There safe and sound, lulled by the backdrop noise of the family's boisterous arguments about who should do what when, I had secretly planned my escape: my moment of freedom.

On the first leg of my venture snug in my comfy train seat watching portly snow flakes descend majestically to mother earth, I was still confident of having a fun adventure. But now standing outside the tawdry bus station, panicking that I had left the paper with the hotel address (which I had prudently decided to locate before I hailed a cab) on my bedroom bureau second thoughts buzzed around me like angry mosquitoes. Loss of the paper threatened to be bad news on two counts: one, having forgotten the name of the hotel I didn't know where to go, and two, if I had left the information at home my family would find it and be after me as swift as hunters after the quick brown fox.

So now, doubts and misgiving started to creep about my legs like mists on the moor. Here I was, free all right: free to freeze. I began to wish that I had stayed home to look after my grandson Teddy, as my daughter-in-law Jenny had suggested.

Only a few weeks earlier, expecting that as usual my calendar would be as empty as the Sahara, Jenny had been including me in her plans. "Mom can look after Teddy," she had announced to the back of my son Tom's head. "It's only a few days." Then, as an afterthought, flashing one of her girlish smiles my way. "You don't mind, do you, mother?"

"Sorry, I can't," I said. "Not that week."

"Why not?" my son tossed over his shoulder, his eyes still glued to the football free-for-all on T.V.

"I'll be out of town."

"With Deb?" Jenny asked. "She never mentioned it."

"No."

Now I had their attention, a rare moment. Tom turned fully around expectantly, Jenny was leaning forward, the newspaper clutched to her chest: "To Maggie's?"

If not to my granddaughter Deb's, then surely I was going to my friend Maggie's. Where else could a 79-year-old woman of limited means go?

Moments like this, which regrettably occur ever more frequently, I want to leap up, pound my chest like Godzilla and roar, "I have a life." There are hundreds of places I could go. My choices have not been whittled down to two. But I remain silent. In fact, two is a stretch.

"I'm going up to Toronto for the weekend," I said.

"With whom? We're going away and Deb is at school."

"With me," I said, attempting to give finality to my tone.

"On your own?"

"You got it," I sang out.

A heavy gauze of silence descended on the room while this unexpected announcement made its way into my son and daughter-in-law's psyche.

"Mother, it's no time to start travelling on your own," my son said in the petulant tone he uses when things go off track: a missed episode of his favorite TV shoot out or no fish and chips on the restaurant menu.

"Tom," Jenny cautioned, as usual to no effect. Son Tom was in full swing.

"You're not thinking of doing something crazy?"

For all but the onset of rheumatism, my son Tom seems to have passed me on the age grid. He is forever concerned about his reputation in the community having landed himself a reasonable job on our non-descript town council and become the director of a small but "up and coming" local firm which produces, of all things, cement garden ornaments. (Who can take anyone seriously who considers gnomes and poorly poured plaster nudes a requisite to a beautiful garden?) A year ago when he discovered me at a local charity concert sporting a new large-patterned red and orange dress, he was so outraged I worried he would have a heart attack.

The revelation that I planned to go to Toronto, thirty miles by train, alone, won me a call from Deb the next day. "Grandma, I didn't know you wanted to go to Toronto. I'll go with you but I'm in the middle of exams. Next month would work. You name the day." Had she been sent as a martyr to the cause or was she just being her kind self?

"Thanks, dear but I am going the week of the 8th and I'm looking forward to going on my own," and added coyly, "You like going places on your own, don't you Deb?"

I could almost hear her searching her mind for a suitable answer. We had been comrades against her father's controlling nature over the years. And now this, "Yes, I do, but, well I am…healthier," she finally said.

But I would not be dissuaded; I wanted to go on an adventure and had come up with the idea from a mystery I read that it would be fun to go to a convention. I heard about a romance writer's to-do in Toronto, open to all, so I signed up on-line. What got me in trouble later was the fact that not only was I not a writer but I had not read any romance novels. The only thing I had ever written was a short poem about the sin of bearing false witness, which I wrote at the age of 14, under the influence of a crush on the local minister's son Jasper. That also went wrong. It turns out Jasper had described me as "a bit of alright body wise" until he read the poem after which he classified me as a sanctimonious ass.

For my adventure, I had chosen a writer's conference. There are not a lot of things you can pretend to be at my age. If I had gone to a gardening convention, I would be expected to know about beetles or the name of those tall spiny purple plants. And I was confident that my acting skills were up to pretending to be a writer, I had been acting the Granny for years with great success. I had selected my travel wardrobe carefully: glamorous, lots of color and flashy jewelry.

To my relief, I finally found the paper with the hotel address, hailed a taxi and headed for the conference center confident my worries were over. After signing in and lugging my suitcase to my room, I changed into my flamboyant red outfit and went to the Meet and Greet room. It was buzzing with delighted delegates all with little Tell Me a Story nametags. Had I joined them, sipped wine and eaten canapés with the rest, all would have been well.

Trouble is I cannot pass up an opportunity for a prize—even those contests that are just a marketing ploy to sell you a time-share in some place you'd never go. When I saw a table with a huge sign offering delegates a chance to win a laptop and weekend at a Spa, over I went. As soon as I filled out our home phone number, I realized I should have given my cell number. Too late, I was grabbed from behind. Oh no, I thought, I've been discovered. Only later did I realize the woman had slyly taken my half competed form with my phone number. At the time, I was scrambling for something to say.

"It's you," the young woman squealed, warmly crushing my arthritic fingers, her voice gurgling with cheeriness. She clearly was delighted to renew my acquaintance but I had no idea who she was. My memory is not as sharp as it used to be, but with the young woman's brilliant red hair, slender figure and Madonna smile, she was not a person you would forget.

"Don't say anything," she whispered to my armpit. "Priscilla Rosebud, I've read everything of yours. I recognized you instantly. You look so like I knew you would."

For once, I was speechless. "Well dear," then noticing the tag, "Gypsy May, I am complimented…"

"I know you're incognito," Gypsy whispered, glancing around surreptitiously. "I won't tell a soul if you promise to have a drink with me later. Mimosa, of course, your favourite." With a leer, and squeeze of the arm, she was off. Rosebud? Was that supposed to be a reference to Citizen Kane? That seemed unlikely.

A drink was needed and quick and no mimosa whatever that was, a good stiff rum and coke. I moved towards what they call a no host bar (a euphemism for 'you pay'), and ordered. When I turned to case the joint, sipping my weak but expensive beverage, I noticed a clump of people in the corner watching me none too subtly—so much for Miss Sealed Lips.

I quickly slipped into the hall, and whipped off my glasses, with which ironically I cannot read, and scanned the program. Oops, there I was, Rosebud, the main speaker the next morning.

This presented a quandary. I had paid my conference fee, and was hungry but hanging about was chancy. As I sidled towards the buffet lunch, I caught people smiling knowingly at me and then one after another they came up to offer drinks. With only two hands I was hard pressed to take all I would have liked to. "I enjoyed your latest," one person hissed. It was like being royalty albeit riskier. If Rosebud were appearing next day surely her agent or someone who'd recognize her, would be around.

What a story to dine out on, I thought, but of course that was only if I could get out alive. Armed with two drinks, one tucked into the side of a plate piled with hors d'œuvres I slipped out on the balcony. I glanced below to witness clusters of people below gesticulating and smiling as if we were part of a conspiracy. I was sorry that I had no hat to wave or perhaps better a helicopter to make a dramatic exit. Then when someone from behind whispered, "I thought she was only about 30?"

This was not one of those moments you could extricate yourself from gracefully. I could hardly announce to the swelling crowd, I am not Rosebud, only to be asked: Who are you? It was time to make a break for it.

I headed for the back door and, fearing I would be caught in the hall, went up to my room, ordered room service, and watched the proceedings on the closed circuit TV. Next day, Rosebud appeared. With her large hat and veil, she could have been me but with stockier legs. I even wondered if she were a he.

On Sunday, when I arrived safely home, chuckling at my adventure, which unfortunately could only be shared with the cat and my friend Maggie, Jenny's eyes told me they needed some news. I confided that

I had gone up to Toronto to buy Christmas gifts. Jenny took my bags, "You old sweet. You're always doing things for us."

Just as I was painfully making my way upstairs, my hand in my pocket fingering the conference tag, Jenny called out to me. "Someone called here looking for a Ms. Rosebud, what an unlikely name. Tom thought you'd know what that was about."

"Me?" I squealed, catching myself before I tumbled down the stairs. "Why me?"

"You're the film buff," she said. "Isn't the term Rosebud from a famous movie?"

(Originally published: *Halfway Down the Stairs*, 2014)

Not Yet 45

As winner of the coveted Billybong Prize for progressive literature, Theresa, not yet 45, should have been on cloud nine. And had her sister not come to the ceremony, young daughter in hand, Theresa having left her worries about her future decision (syllable or one letter story?) at home would have basked in the glory.

As the event unfolded, all eyes were on her: perched proudly in a stylish new turquoise dress, face modestly composed. The celebrities, there to honour her, were lined up ready to perform as soon as the emcee finished his laudatory remarks.

Theresa's husband, delighted with the monetary award, had attended with pleasure and promptly dozed off. But at the sound of the first speaker shouting Theresa's winning piece, he suddenly jerked awake.

At the second 'reading' her niece leapt up and cried out.

"Why's he saying that bad word?"

The child's mother, grimaced apologetically to the stunned audience, and hissed at her daughter to be silent but to no avail. At the next recitation, the small sharp voice bellowed, "Why are people going up and saying that rude word in funny voices?"

The audience, until that moment reverently waiting to discover how the next celebrity would read the winning 'piece,' gasped.

Earlier the Emcee had proclaimed, "I call this innovative new genre a 'piece.' In her creation our winner, like Michael Angelo, has scrapped the irrelevant from the stone slab to reveal the masterpiece hidden inside: the nugget that illuminates a response to our troubled times. No easy task."

That was putting it mildly, thought Theresa. Years earlier, when her first novel had received negative reviews, ('lugubrious' had been one critic's stinging word) Theresa had turned to short stories. 'Interminable' had been one remark. Flash fiction had been her next foray. Under 1000 words she still didn't get the fulsome praise she sought. She whittled down to 800, then 500 and finally to 50 words. But now her moment had arrived.

Six months earlier awakened at night by what one critic called a 'prosian revelation,' Theresa had leapt from bed and rushed to her computer. Fortunately, she discovered there was still time to enter a submission for The Billybong Prize. With her inspiration, it was within reach. She paced the floor, drank wine, glared out the window, and absent-mindedly attacked dust bunnies while searching for the 'word.' It had to be powerful, daring, and evocative: a word to reflect the times.

Suddenly inspired, Theresa stumbled to the computer, signed on the Billybong site and off went her gem. Two months later, the congratulatory phone call, and here she was.

Following her niece's outburst, there was a hush in the room. The Emcee attempted to laugh it off. "Children" he said. "What do they know of art?"

The celebrity at the podium, primed to speak the piece, looked at the hostile faces in front of him. In a small voice, quite unlike the one he had practiced by the hour in front of his mirror, he whispered, "Fuck."

(Originally published: *Sybil*, March, 2020)

The Wrong Box

New in town, Walter was delighted to be one of four locals invited to give a presentation on what the facilitator called his "profession" to the high school graduates. Chadville was obviously more appreciative of his type of work than was his former town, where they called a long haul trucker's work just a "blue collar job."

When he'd filled out the address form for the Welcome Lady, Walter had explained that he'd retired from his demanding work because he was no longer alert enough to do it safely. "If I keep trucking I'll put other people's lives at risk," he said and the woman had sung out, "You've picked a great place to retire but don't expect us to call you doctor or sir. All first names here."

Walter was fine with that. He certainly wasn't a doctor and had never in his life been called sir. But informal or not, he was pleased someone recognized the role of the trucker. He would enjoy explaining the challenges of his work: long, lonely hours but good money, especially for someone who'd hardly scraped through grade 12.

"Here goes," he thought noting it was his turn to speak. He pulled his snug sweater over his expanding waist, and prepared to move to the podium.

"Last but not least I'm proud to introduce Dr. Walter Bangels, who also demonstrates the importance of a university degree."

As one who had never even eaten in a University cafeteria let alone attended a university, Walter gasped. What had he said to the Welcome Lady to give her the impression he was a doctor? In retrospect he realized he hadn't actually said he was a trucker but he surely hadn't suggested he was a doctor. His eyes flashed to the program where his name appeared in neon: Dr. Walter Bangels. When filling out the form for the welcome lady, he'd obviously ticked off the wrong box—Dr. not Mr.—and so she'd concluded he was a physician.

This could be a tricky. He'd have to rely on some jokes to keep the crowd entertained. Thankfully, at the luncheon earlier, he hadn't suggested what the principal should do about his unsightly rash nor discussed his lighthearted approach to open-heart surgery.

(Originally published: *The Short Humour Site*, 2016)

The Last Laugh

For once, the locals agreed: the way the four old timers behaved at Dickie Wainwright's funeral was appalling. What could have fired up four guys who could hardly rouse themselves to check if they'd won the lottery, to take such action?

No one who had seen the foursome crunched together in the second pew "like miscast extras from an old western," had imagined what they'd get up to. They had appeared a docile line-up. The dude stuffed near the wall was decked out in a shiny black suit ten years out of style, the next one sported a plaid shirt that had been ironed 'til the creases cut, the third wore an ill fitting beige jacket attempting by the strength of one faltering button to cover his expansive belly and finally the dresser, as he was known by his drinking buddies, was slicked out in a blazer and white pants anticipating that June would perk up for the funeral.

Regret might have been expected on the faces of four men who had known the deceased since high school and there might have been a trace of that but not so much on behalf of their drinking buddy's demise as for themselves. If a buddy, who like themselves had only gone 65, had bit the dust, would they be next?

But even stronger than their discomfort at the grim reaper's slash was their guilt. From the moment that Freddie, the bartender at the Pickled Oats, had announced to the Thursday night regulars that Dickie had died, regrets and excuses had flowed over the foursome as chilling as spring creek water.

"We should have done something sooner." "How were we to know he wasn't conning us again" "Yeah, after bragging for years about his health, who'd believe he was sick?"

Then one of the four piped up that they had done a lot for Dickie and another reminded them how much they'd lost at poker. Their heads bobbed as they fell over one another to list their many kindnesses and losses when, two months earlier, they had finally conceded that Dickie was a very sick guy.

"I lent him $200 towards a high end snowmobile I couldn't afford for myself," the dresser hissed under his breathe, "money I will never see again."

"Last February in that storm where 17 cars went off the highway, I drove him to town to pick it up," said plaid shirt.

"After he got sick, we never let him buy a round."

"As if he ever tried."

"And we played poker with him, the supposed learner, even though he kept cleaning us out."

"Yeah, but as he said, with *his* health he had to be lucky at something."

The night before the funeral, slouched at their customary pub table, the foursome had rehashed the scenario so many times they'd gotten tangled in the narrative.

Since they'd married, every Thursday they met at the Pickled Oats from 7 to 10 p.m. After a drink or two, they'd talk about how the world was going to hell in a hand basket; and how they suffered on the home front: the wives were making them lose weight, stop smoking, exercise, drink less beer, not watch TV sports and a hundred other injustices. And uninvited, but as punctual as tax time, came a number five—Dickie Wainwright .

Beer in hand, he'd regale them with his present, past and future exploits. And by the end of the evening somehow, one or more of the four had agreed to lend him his lawnmower or thirty bucks or bought into some new fangled get rich scheme. They figured that over the years they'd lost about $6,000—a lot to this pack—in beer, food and loans; and free services from one mechanic, one roofer, one gardener and a delivery guy.

Dickie always had the last word. Whenever the guys mentioned a high point in their week: a chance to snooze at work, a good buy at the flea market, an escape from a mother-in-law, or a sale on beer, Dickie outdid them with tales of his prowess. He'd conned them so many times over the years: get rich schemes they couldn't lose money on, but did; money for his son's trumpet, which the kid never played; a trip to Florida to see his dying mom, who turned out to have died ten years earlier. "But for memories boys, for memories," he explained when they confronted him.

Finally the dresser's wife told them to smarten up and printed off suggestions from a website about how to say 'no.' After a few false starts with someone missing a signal: "What's wrong with your eyebrows?" "What are you wiggling your mouth about?" They had set up a sort of code to warn the others when Dickie was conning them.

Then five months ago, after years bragging about his health, Dickie had moved from healthiest to sickest. He one-upped every mention of a sore hip or stomach ailment with a description of his more exotic illnesses. Knowing Dickie, they were skeptical. For two months as Dickie described how Dr. Conway and the many specialists he had consulted were flummoxed by his rare ailments they refused to believe a word.

"Might be the last favour I'll ever ask you," Dickie would sigh asking for help with a backed up toilet, or "Who knows if I'll make it to next week," he'd say noting that he wanted the roof tiles replaced before he died so widow Cindy wouldn't be flooded out. The most pressing demand was that they play poker with him, so as he put it "he could take his mind off his imminent demise."

Then one Wednesday, on a visit to the dentist, plaid shirt saw Dickie leaving Dr. Conway's building and a week later, his wife saw Dickie slip into the medical building and the foursome concluded Dickie wasn't pulling their leg after all.

* * *

When they arrived for the funeral and spied Dr. Conway they decided to show their appreciation for his efforts.

The dresser sidled up to him and whispered, "Thanks from us all for all you did. He counted on you."

The doctor looked over and winked, "Well, he did learn a few tricks."

"Not your fault he succumbed to his disease."

"He died in bed…a heart attack."

"But through his last months when he needed a doc on hand?"

The doctor yanked his arm free of the dresser, "I've got to get inside. I'm going to set the record straight. Who knows what BS that silver tongued preacher will say? "

A shiver of dread passed over the four. Once seated they agonized whether the "something to set the record straight" would be about them—friends who didn't believe when a buddy was sick. How in his hour of need, Dickie's buddies doubted him.

"The heart attack got him in the end," said creases. "But the paper should have said 'after struggling with a long illness.'"

All through the service, the four agonized over what the doctor would say. They hardly heard the sluggish hymns or Dickie's son's remark about his Dad never getting to the mountain he wanted to climb. And finally, the old Doc struggled up to the podium, fumbled with his glasses and gave a wink. "Well," he said, "You probably wonder why I'm here. Until his death, Dickie never had a sick day in his life."

There was an uneasy wave of chuckles from the congregation and the four friends pulled up to straight. "For the last year," the doctor continued, "Dickie and I played poker at my office and even though he always had an Ace up his sleeve, I showed him a trick or two, which, he said, paid off with the boys. " At this the doctor swept his hand to the second pew and caught the astounded faces of the four bar flies.

Plaid shirt shot up. "Are you saying Dickie wasn't sick these last months?"

"He was not," said the Doc, chuckling. "More like him and I'd be out of business."

"Well, I'll be damned," said the dresser, "the old bugger." He leaped up and rushed towards the coffin. Swatting aside the pile of bouquets, he grabbed his own offering, bought on sale and wilting fast. As quick as black flies to the neck, the other three musketeers rushed to do the same.

The congregation gasped, unsure if this was part of the ceremony, as out the door the four went, swinging their bouquets like sabers, and spattering the astonished onlookers with petals. Quick as lightening, down the street they marched, straight to the Pickled Oats.

(Originally published: *The Write Place at the Right Time*, 2011)

Shepherds in Love

Huddled under a grungy blanket, a threat of rain in the air, and a stomach grumbling in response to her wolfing down a can of baked beans, Betty regretted where 'interesting' had gotten her. Across from her, looking as pleased as a lottery winner, Trevor sat, head back, grinning at the stars through the open window. "Who would have ever dreamt that I would meet my soul mate at a party of boring neighbours?"

Who indeed thought Betty, incensed at Tanya for getting her into this fix? A month earlier, she and her ex-friend had been sitting in their favorite back booth at Sprinklers (toasty and odor free), drinking Red Rose tea, when her friend floated the idea that set Betty on her downward spiral.

To that point in the meal Betty had been musing about the choice between mushroom or tomato soup for supper when Tanya's information set her thinking more profound thoughts. In response to Betty's complaint that it was hard to attract or keep interesting guys, her friend had advised.

"It's 'cause you're too normal. You need a special quirk. Who wants someone who's perfect?"

"Me," she'd replied. "Regular, down to earth guy: good paying job, never married, wants a small family, romantic and handsome."

"That's another problem. You should be looking for someone who is interesting but not perfect. That would be attainable. And show that you also have some tiny transgression, some sin from the past, some strange hobby or interest or obsession.

"I like you because we've friends for years," continued Tanya, "But when you meet up with a guy, he probably thinks, well she's predictable."

"Predictable?" Betty scoffed, "Who knows what soup I might have tonight: mushroom or tomato?"

"But not buffalo," her friend had said making Betty wonder where you could even buy buffalo soup.

On her walk home—through the park as usual—Betty tried to think of some past transgression, but she had always lived by the book, and kept herself out of harm's way. She'd have to develop an unusual hobby or obsession.

"It should be close to the wire," Tanya had insisted, "But not illegal or dangerous, something with a loop hole."

Two nights later at a party, Betty had spied a shy guy lurking in the corner. Earlier she'd noticed her friend's knitting book with a couple of contented looking sheep on the cover (rather a sheep than a chicken, she'd thought). She wondered about shepherds, were there still such people?

She raised herself to full height and sailed towards the corner. Soon she and Trevor, the shy man, were snug against the wall, grabbing hors d'oeuvres as they went past. Trevor had confided that he was single and his last girl friend had lied to him. Because of his family history he had, as he described it, "almost an obsession against liars." Betty agreed particularly in light of the recent acceptance of alternate facts from the high and mighty in the USA."

Just as she thought things were going well and she'd begun describing her clerical job, she noticed that Trevor's eyes were floating around the room.

Remembering Tanya's advice Betty blurted. "I'm a bank teller but I always wanted to be a shepherd."

Trevor swung towards her, grasped her arms, spilling her drink but with a joyous smile. "You did. How wonderful, so did I. We're soul mates."

"Unfortunately I had to give up that dream," she sighed startled by his response.

"Never too late," he cried, "You could still do it. Together we can. Let's get out of here. Get a coffee and check out possibilities on the Internet."

"Sure a coffee," she said, wondering where this would lead.

"My uncle has a few acres in the interior," Trevor said, pulling her behind him. "I've saved a bit of money. Let's find where we could get a few sheep. Shepherd entrepreneurs."

And then everything moved at break-neck speed. The call to the Uncle—rousted from bed—ended up with the old man's refrain "Have you been drinking" and finally "Call me at 7 a.m. tomorrow if you're really interested."

And here she was four weeks later. Sure, Trevor was handsome, exuberant, and complimentary: "I knew you were an animal lover and a potential entrepreneur," he had enthused, "And gorgeous to boot."

Surely a dilapidated cabin and five sheep wasn't what they meant by the term entrepreneur, Betty thought pulling her sweater around her shoulders and over her nose to avoid the overpowering reek of wet sheep.

"Of course we don't need to spend our whole lives doing this," she suggested wondering how she was going to pay off the loan her mother had given her. The money was supposed to pay for two courses at the local community college not the hind end of an ewe! She hadn't dared say to Mr. Hates Liars that she had been…well lying about her shepherd aspirations.

"Don't have to but love to," Trevor crowed. "I'm only sorry we've only one life," he cried, and hugged her to him. Taking a deep breath as he leaned against her, he enthused, "You smell wonderful but you're right, we should have a side line."

"A side-line?" she asked, hopefully.

"Yes sheep by-products, like sheep soap and perfume: a line of goods like movie stars have." He leaned back and stretched his arms to the sides, engulfing her. "What a lucky day when we met. How could I ever guess I would meet such a truthful and loving woman like you? Sexy and smart and best of all a fellow sheep lover."

"Yes, how could you have guessed?" Betty said wondering how you could even make sheep perfume and if you did, who'd buy it.

(Originally published: *The Short Humour Site*, 2018)

The McLean Boys and that Wild Alex Hare

I sailed into the meeting, the first since my two weeks off, expecting to be cheered for my negotiating skills, but was met instead with a sea of grim faces.

"Didn't the trade go through?" I asked. "Isn't the menace gone?"

"He's gone alright," said the chairperson. "But in exchange we got someone worse."

"Not another brother?"

"No. The wild one."

The week before I left on holiday we'd had a meeting at which we had finally decided to get rid of the whiner.

As usual we were clustered around fluffy white tables, enjoying a break and beefing about clients who moaned about their fate: the whiner being the worst.

"I wish he'd been sent to hell," said one disgruntled worker. Nods all around.

"As if we could choose who goes where," said the trainee.

"It's not as if the proper procedures aren't followed," grumbled another.

"So today the usual complaint from the McLean boy?" asked the chairperson who never had to serve on the Complaints Desk.

"Yeah, whine, whine, whine."

" 'Why are we called the McLean Boys without first names and Hare is called the Wild Alex Hare? Why is he the only one who's wild?' "

"Did you explain we had no authority on earth?"

"Of course, for the 25th time."

"I blame this on the wipe out. The technology they were using last century was so bad people could remember things."

"Worse still they seem to be able to hear what is going on down below."

"Yeah. He's read all the books and seen the movie. He wants to be the star but is only a walk-on."

"So is there anything we can do to shut him up?"

"No. But if the boys ended up here why wasn't Wild Alex Hare sent here?"

"He was sent back to earth for another round. Hoping he would be less wild."

"And was he?"

"Well less violent and in a more acceptable way. He was a minister of the Church of Forgiveness. "

"So he didn't kill people?"

"Only if they came unto his property but mostly he just slept with their wives."

"And in the trade we got him?"

"Yeah, he ended up below but they decided to trade him."

"We keep asking for a check on who is being traded but we just end up with whoever they want to get rid of."

"And I can see why they wanted to get rid of him."

"He's already been at the Complaints Desk five times in four days."

"And what is his complaint?"

"Hates harp music, argues adultery should be a sin so he shouldn't have been traded and doesn't want to be the same place as the McLean boys."

"Well so what to do?"

"Why not put the four of them somewhere where they can fight it out?"

"Sure. What about the middle waiting room?"

"I thought the pen was shut down in an austerity move."

"Austerity be damned, I say we open it back up."

(Originally published: *Corner Bar Magazine*, 2019)

For The Love of a Leg

Charles or the leg, which was it to be? Charles was difficult to live with, often a negative naysayer. The leg, on the other hand, was an easy partner, and offered comfort in difficult times. It was there for her when she returned home on the boil following a rancid work meeting, there when Charles droned on about why her ideas were impractical, there when the world entire hurtled towards environmental and social disasters.

But her dear leg was more than a comfort in hard times; it also glorified good times. Now when she got a "hats off" from the boss, a seat on the bus, a wink from a stranger, her success was appreciated on the home front. At those times, cradled in her hand, the leg's warmth and reliable firmness shot electric possibilities surging down her arm.

Since the tiny leg appeared (as with most great loves, unexpected and unsought) her life became more doable, her confidence soared; there was a lilt to her walk. Armed with its presence, she was impermeable to the stings and arrows of outrageous fortune, even to Charles' nasty comments. Then came high noon.

For years, Charles and she had shared a home office where they reigned together peaceably, each at his or her own desk. Charles had ignored the mementoes Alice displayed around her computer until the fatal day the innocent appendage caught his eye and sent him spinning. Suddenly, with her husband's jealous intervention, the leg's existence was in peril.

"What the hell is that thing?" Charles said sweeping it up from the small tray where it lay cradled among her multi-colored paper clips.

"Leave it," she warned.

"It's a tiny leg," he said incredulously.

It was indeed. A small, translucent plastic leg from, one assumed, an equally miniature skeleton. She had found it, abandoned, on the beach.

"Where'd you get it?"

"Leave it," she said ramming her husband aside. "I don't touch things on your desk." She would have added "except spare change and gum," had she been in a conciliatory mood.

Charles would have flung the leg into the garbage had she not, like a mother bird guarding her chick, pounced on the predator hawk. The beloved leg safely gripped in her hand, they stared at one another across the chasm.

It was a narrow chasm as their shared office—advertised as a 2nd bedroom when they bought the condo—was too cramped for any but elves to sleep in. The room did, however, serve the two of them comfortably as a workspace: two desks, two chairs and a shared bookcase. But was it big enough for three?

"This is an office," Charles said. "I don't want clients finding bodily parts strew about."

"It wasn't strewn. It was snug in its container."

"It's like those limbs pilgrims hang in churches," he cried. "Your Catholicism is rearing its ugly head."

"What about that monstrosity?" Alice roared shaking her finger at the framed mosaic creation displayed prominently over Charles' desk.

"That's my Nannie Buffs' art. In spite of the cracked glass from your rough treatment it's a beauty."

"And this?" Alice said opening her hand to exhibit the delicate gem leg sparkling in the sun.

"Al-Al-Al-ice," he pumped. "You cannot compare a plastic toy part with Nannie's art: she was a missionary in Africa, for God's sake.

Alice stared up at the monstrosity of glass, beads, and plastic, roughly shaped into a ship and stuck on a backdrop of faded blue velvet. A beam of light flashed on the broken glass, awakening in Alice an epiphany.

"I'll have the glass replaced this week," she said, "Promise."

Charles looked at her suspiciously, "And the leg?"

"You've seen the last of it."

Alice lifted down the framed art piece and blowing a kiss into her hand swept out the door.

Three days later, when Charles returned from line dancing, Nannie Buffs' art piece shone clearly through a glass hung over his desk.

"They did a good job," he admitted, pleased to see Alice had seen the light. "It never looked better."

"I agree," said Alice, gazing past Charles to her true love, which shone like a cut diamond masthead, and was shaped cunningly like a leg.

(Originally published: *InfectiveNK,* 2014)

First Prize for Fight-Free

Penny climbed unto the platform squeezing her flowered dress to her side to prevent the wind blowing it over her head. Her day had arrived. She was a winner, ready for the crown—albeit only a paper Mache one—but even more important, ready for the cash prize.

As had been pointed out from a critic at a recent town council meeting, the podium (where the ceremony was taking place) was constructed such that it resembled a medieval gallows. But unlike at a hanging, the crowd wasn't cheering. Even at this late date, the other contestants—who Penny considered suspicious poor losers—were jealous and might try to grasp victory from her.

Mayor Higgins sidled over to her and hissed, "Where the hell is Fred?"

"Had a turn for the worse, but here in spirit."

"Forget spirit. Get the lazy bugger over here and fast."

As usual, Penny's husband presented a challenge. But she wasn't going to let him dampen the proudest moment of her life: the prizewinner in a competition that most couples in town had contended.

Prior to this day, Penny had never won a prize—except the basket of food from the Cats Are Us pet store (which even their dog had refused to eat).

The present competition had been sponsored by Wellness Times Two—a local counseling service—in response to a regional newspaper report naming Bucksville, with more marital disputes per capita than any other town in the country, "The Fightingest Town in the North."

Local couples were competing to be fight free the longest; the last contestants standing were to be the winners. The initial reward had been increased by the town's funeral parlor and was now over $4,000 bucks. In a small town, with half of the locals laid-off when the Better Bows' jobs moved to China that was nothing to sneeze at.

The hitch was that the crowd couldn't believe Penny and Fred were the winners. Over the years, the couple had attained a local notoriety for the volume and intensity of their arguments.

When the contest began, local folks had tried to catch she and Fred squabbling. For the first few weeks it was a terrible challenge. If someone heard angry shouts and recorded them or caught Penny and Fred out the back yard arguing about fish livers or fertilizers, the couple would have been disqualified in a flash. But no one had. After years of swiping at one another as if they were mosquitoes, they had lived peacefully, as far as could be heard from outside the home, since the day they signed on as contestants.

"Needs must," she said to her friend Mable.

It helped that Fred wasn't getting out like he used to, and that she spent most days hunkered down at the library. And they both were solid sleepers afternoons and evenings, which cut down the opportunities for quarrels.

"I thought the contest was crazy," Mable had admitted, "But if it brought you and Fred together, it wasn't all bad."

"All good in fact," said the loving wife.

"How is he anyhow? The back still bothering him?"

"No, but he does have other health issues."

Since the contest began, the locals who had signed on had tried desperately to keep from arguing and focused on catching others who couldn't hold their tongues. But finally one by one, often with goading from neighbours, couples had been disqualified and only Penny and Fred remained in the race. Now it was time for their crowning moment; Fred was the only fly in the ointment.

The crowd, roasting in the afternoon sun, shouted at Mayor Higgins to get a move on; they were anxious to tuck into the promised back-ribs and beer offered by Eat More Foods.

Finally, unable to persuade her to hustle home and drag Fred back to the event, Mayor Higgins plopped the crown on Penny's head and announced. "As Penny's better half isn't here, I'll hold the check. They can pick it up at City Hall."

Grumbling about the injustices she faced, Penny hurried home to reread the contest rules. Surely she could get by on a technicality.

"You've screwed us up again, Fred," she said to her husband. "I've already booked my tickets for Hawaii. *You* never think how your actions affect others."

In frustration, she reeled off the many times her husband had not been there for her. For once, Fred didn't high tail it down to the corner pub to avoid her [illegible]

Finally, she was forced to shut the lid on him. Even at the best of times, the cellar wasn't warm, and this afternoon the cool air from the freezer was giving her a particular chill.

(Originally published: *Foliate Oak Literary Magazine*, 2016)

Dancing Shoes

Tom laughed indulgently when his friend Frank apologized for having only a quick pint. "Bette and I are going dancing tonight. You and Myrna should join us."

"No way," Tom said. "It's been so long since I went dancing with Myrna that she doesn't even bother to ask any more. If I weakened now, we'd be back at square one."

"We used to have fun, the four of us."

True, in times gone by Tom had waltzed his wife around the floor but only with a view to whirling her into his arms permanently. Since the wedding march ten years earlier, there was no dancing for him. Now he only marched.

The fact was he was more a military man than a dancing man. Not military in the sense that he had been in the army, although, as a high school cadet, he had paraded around a muddy field one summer. He was a military man in the sense that he liked order, insisted Myrna iron his drip-dry shirts, and keep everything ship-shape. Imagination was, to him, a potion best left in the bottle. He had no patience for fantasy. Second fact was he only did things that served a purpose and now that he and Myrna were hooked, dancing served no purpose.

"If you want to stay home stuck in front of the TV, send Myna on her own, his friend said. "There's lots of singles."

"No way."

"Maybe she's already found a new guy."

"Old Myrna? No chance."

"Last week at the supermarket, she had a flushed, in-love look."

"Well, it's not with me."

"I'm sure it isn't," his friend said, which ruffled Tom's feathers.

A few days earlier, their neighbor with the yapping Collie had called over the fence to Myrna, "What are you up to? You look great." In reply, his wife giggled in a way Tom hadn't heard in ten years.

What was going on? Recently, everyone who saw Myrna commented how good she was looking—their son said it, her best friend noted it, and now even Frank who hardly noticed any woman over 30—which Myrna was far past—was joining the chorus.

When Tom decided to look for himself, he noticed his wife hadn't gained the pounds he had since they walked down the aisle. Her face had sort of a pink blush (probably some new makeup) and her energy level was high (those vitamins). But the small puffs under her eyes gave her away.

Of course, the idea of her having a suitor was crazy. Myrna and he worked in the same cramped office and she wasn't out of his sight for more than 30 minutes during the day.

And her age was showing… He confronted her about sneaking a nap before supper; he couldn't understand how she needed more sleep. Regular as clockwork, they both bunked down at ten. Tom had a solid routine that involved a facemask, earplugs, a sleeping pill, and loose flannel pajamas. Myrna refused to follow his routine. "I sleep fine and I like the feel of my silk night dress."

"Looks more like a day dress to me," he grumbled. "And what's happening with these slippers?"

"What do you mean, what's happening?"

"I knew they'd be impractical when you suggested them for your Christmas gift. It's only March and they're worn out."

"I wear them; that's why."

"For an hour a day in the house, hardly enough to wear them down like that. I should write the company. Where is the bill anyhow?"

"Never mind."

Tom had grumbled to Frank about the slippers, they weren't cheap—bought at that new boutique on 5th Street and three months later they were in tatters.

"Maybe she dances at night." Frank said.

"Sure—to the bathroom."

"It's like the dancing princesses."

"The what?"

"You know that fairy tale where the princesses sneak out and dance all night?"

"I don't read fairy tales."

"But when Becky was little, didn't you read to her?"

"Myrna did the reading. Anyhow what would be open after 10 at night?"

"Get serious, half the town is open after ten: Becker's Ballroom, The Commodore, the Chunky Chilly."

Tom scoffed at the ridiculous idea, but that night he studied Myrna carefully. He observed her as she chewed her chicken, scrutinized her as she brushed her teeth and hung around the door when she answered a phone call ("just a salesman," she said, but obviously a chatty one).

Finally, Myra turned on him. "What?" she said, her eyes popping. "Is my face dirty?"

"Can't a guy look at his wife," Tom said, trying for one of his charming smiles, now somewhat rusty.

"It sounds crazy," he said to Frank. "But could she be sneaking out at night?"

"The way you sleep, she could be driving a tank through your bedroom. When we were in Vegas, we played poker at the end of your bed and you never noticed."

That did it. Action was required. Friday night Tom planned his first reconnaissance to survey the field. Once Myrna dozed off, Tom moved a chair from the corner to the hallway and hunkered down. It was hard to keep awake. When he thought dawn had finally arrived, he checked his watch to find it was only 11:49. The next time he woke, it was morning and his neck was so stiff he was lopsided. Myrna was still sleeping but he noticed her slippers had moved to the end of the bed.

The next day, Frank told him about their friend Manny whose wife was divorcing him. "Said he was pulling her down, she wanted to spend the money they got from the house on a long holiday."

Tom scoffed. "He was sleeping at the wheel."

"Guess so. By the time he noticed something was up, she already had Mark Becker for a lawyer."

"Mark Becker?" cried Tom. Even he knew that Mark was the best divorce lawyer in town. If Becker got his hands on you, he would clean you out. It was time for serious action. "The best defense is an offense," he called to Frank as he headed out of the pub.

That night Tom sailed in the door with a pot of mums, purchased at the corner store and still with considerable blooms. "Let's go out dancing," he said to his wife, sweeping her, broom and all, around the hall.

"You hate dancing," she said sweetly, "You don't have to take me dancing."

"I don't like dancing generally," he agreed. "But dancing with you is something special." He got that line from a men's magazine at the dentist. You could use it for anything.

"Well," said Myrna, "...if you insist. But I don't want you to do anything you don't want to."

The specter of Mark Becker hung in the door as Tom remembered that Manny had had to sell his vintage motorcycle.

"I want to. I want to," Tom sang out. "And let's do it regular like Frank and Bette."

He pulled out his wallet—he was on a roll—and shoved a wad of money intended for lottery tickets, into Myrna's hand. "You'll need new slippers," he crowed, "Yours are worn out."

Who could leave a hubby who was so generous? he thought.

Myrna hurried into the bedroom and returned with a Christmas-wrapped box. "Those worn-down slippers are old ones I got from my sister," she said happily. "I saved the ones you gave me in case you changed your mind about dancing," she continued with a wink. "And you did."

(Originally published: *The Write Place at the Write Time*, 2012)

Kids, Cats and Quick Exits

For Larry, choosing between Trixie and his balloons was the most wrenching decision he had ever faced. Trixie was close to perfection with her bouncy blond curls, soar in the sky smile and understanding heart. He'd do anything for her, anything that is but give up his balloons.

He had collected his first balloon (long since interred) years earlier, the day he bought the house. A sizeable basement room was now dedicated to them. They needed the entire room because Larry could not—and who but a heartless thug could—kill them. No matter how old and weak a balloon got, the thin pastel plastic stretched and bulging, he couldn't pierce it.

Others did. When his former friend Tom discovered an elderly balloon from Fred's retirement party hiding behind a chair at work, he squeezed it to death. And then, to Larry's horror, he'd thrown the balloon in the garbage as if it were nothing.

Not Larry, even when they finally did die—like people their life expectancy had increased in recent years—Larry gave them a proper send off. After their last gasp, they were sorted by color or design so they could be with their own, and placed in a small metal box by his window.

Now he was faced with a choice: Trixie or his balloons. Struggle as he might, Larry couldn't come up with any way to save his balloons and meet Trixie's three points of contention: kids, cats and speedy exits. First, Trixie wanted kids, and he wasn't against it. If he had five hands he would sign up. But as it was when they went for a walk, his two hands were occupied: Trixie with one hand, his balloon with the other. Having lost his first love—a red helium balloon—he was terrified of losing another love—Trixie.

The cliché about the first love being the strongest was true. His was a shiny red balloon with a thin golden ribbon and so plump he could hardly get his arms around it. As soon as the balloon had been bestowed on him, Larry had lost interest in the birthday party: the other children swooping around playing airplane, the treat bags stuffed with plastic toys and gummy candies, the mothers clucking that it was time to leave. He'd raced outside, swinging his balloon, which in the breeze was as wild as he. It tugged to be free, to join the clouds. He hurried ahead of his mother who hesitated to shout thanks to Mrs. Bean and then called to him, "Larry, careful, hold on, hold on."

As he turned towards her, his hand opened and whoosh his everything exploded into the air. "Mommy," he cried in horror watching, his heart rising. "Mommy, get it."

The small Larry jumped and stretched his thin arms as far as he could but the balloon was already flying high. He watched in horror as it shrunk smaller and smaller.

"Mommy," he cried angrily, "Get my balloon." His mother put her arm around his bony shoulder, "It's gone, Larry."

"I want it back," he said stamping his feet on the icy sidewalk.

"It's gone to play with the clouds," she said.

Larry stared into the sky stretching his head so far back it threatened to snap off. "Come back, come back. I want you, Balloon," he cried in his fierce thin voice but it refused to come back. Instead, it got tinier and tinier until it was the size of a marble and disappeared.

Years had passed since that terrible event but still whenever Larry left the house with his chosen balloon he held it tight and as he also loved Trixie, he held her tight too. Of course, she was too heavy to float away but he could hardly show more concern for his balloon than for his ladylove.

In the early days when he took Trixie's hand as they left the house, she swung his arm and cried, "We're like Parisian lovers walking along Rileyville streets hand in hand." Recently, however, she sometimes tried to break loose in order to window shop or to dash across the street to talk with a friend.

But back to the problem of kids. Larry wasn't against the idea of having them but if he and Trixie had a kid he'd want to hold his or her hand and that would mean giving up Trixie's hand and if he had two kids or twins, well that would be impossible. They could never leave the house.

In a sense, he had his kids, there in the basement. But that was another problem: space. Trixie argued, "We wouldn't have to move. The baby could have the basement room." If so, where were his balloons supposed to go?

When Trixie wasn't talking kids, she was talking cats. Another no-no. If they had a cat, and it got into the basement it might bang the balloons around or rip their lives from them with its sharp claws. No way, no animals.

He had tried to address Trixie's third concern: slow exits. "You're so poky leaving the house," she complained. "I'm tired of pacing the pavement waiting for you, rain or shine."

His mother had sided with Trixie, suggesting he plan ahead. But how could he? He never knew what the day would be like. For example, his red shirt might look good with the yellow balloon in the dim light of the basement (he had tried to install better lights but they didn't help). But then once he got outside, he could see that his outfit didn't do the yellow balloon credit; somehow the light was too bright or too dull. Other times as soon as they got outside he noted the wind, and realized he had brought a balloon that was too large or shaped such that it would struggle in the breeze and the whole afternoon would be spent tugging and yanking and no one would enjoy that.

"Bloody twenty minutes yesterday and fifteen today," Trixie said. "You can leave on time for work."

Of course he could. Workdays he only had to choose a balloon to match his orange overalls—standard uniform at Buckley's—and the balloon would be mostly indoors so he didn't have to worry about strong winds.

So those were the issues: kids, cats and quick exits. He and Trixie had fought around and around this mulberry bush for four weeks until yesterday when Trixie threatened that if he didn't budge by morning, she was gone. Her suitcase (tissue paper between the layers of clothes to avoid creases) placed by the door, spoke of her determination.

The previous night had been the worst of Larry's life. He loved Trixie, with her perky nose and a laugh that would stop a van, but what would life be without his balloons? In the small hours, unable to sleep, he had visited the balloons a number of times. (He watched them in the dim nightlight, not putting on the overhead light, which would disturb their rest.) As he opened their door, they rustled and shifted about, restless in their sleep just like Trixie often was. That's something he'd miss if she left, her moving quietly beside him, the warmth of her soft haired arm across his chest and the curve of her back as she cuddled against him. But it was too late for second thoughts; it was morning. Trixie had seen his note and she was moving around upstairs. The basement door creaked opened.

"That's it, Larry," she shouted. "This is goodbye"

He was stung. He couldn't bear to climb the stairs to see her off. He'd left a note to say he loved her but that just like the movie stars their differences were "irreconcilable."

Standing with his balloons around him like a multicolored skirt—Larry peered out the grimy basement window. Trixie's feet jogged down the front stairs and headed up the walk. She was wearing her favourite "cheer me up" red high heals and his breath caught as he watched the tiny heels clip away. When she got to the sidewalk, she turned back—would she relent? No, she just shrugged.

Behind him, in loving support, his balloons clustered—all ages, all shapes, and all colors. Had it not been for their constancy, he couldn't have faced Trixie's departure.

He reached out his hand to caress his new silver Congratulations balloon, so cool to the touch. Over his shoulder he glimpsed his elderly Thanks balloon loyal and resplendent in gold and green.

Down the street Trixie tripped along, her shiny crimson shoes getting smaller and smaller just like that fateful red balloon had done those many years ago. Finally, all he could see were the heels and then nothing.

He'd always intended to make a contingency plan for his balloons in case of his death. Now that Trixie was gone, he'd move that to the top of his list.

(Originally published: *Foliate Oak Literary Magazine*, 2013.)

Funeral Chat

In response to Fred's question, "What'll I say at your funeral?" Chunker, who was slumped over a pint of the cheapest, jerked up and asked, "Am I dying?"

"After today's fiasco, I want to plan ahead," Fred said. "As your best friend, I'll be a speaker at your gig."

"Don't call it a gig, that sounds too cheerful."

"Whatever, I'll be center stage."

"You're right, Janet will be overcome with grief and my ex, Betsy, won't come back from wherever to gloat."

"So, I want to be ready."

"It's creepy to imagine my obit waiting in your underwear drawer."

"No way. It'll be in my desk with my bills."

"Still, it'll be set to go."

"Why not, newspapers have famous celebs' obits on the ready."

"Famous I'm not. And anyhow what makes you think I'll be first out?"

"Maybe not. I'm also leaving notes for my service. Danny Boy for a song."

"No way, that's too sad. We'll need something upbeat."

"My funeral, my choice. You do agree Bert's funeral was a bust?"

"Yeah. He's lucky he missed it. Who was the dude who spoke?"

"A guy who runs the curling rink. Bert's wife got the place rent free if he could pitch the place."

"So that's why he plugged curling."

"And didn't mention Bert's wives."

"You mean other than Merle?"

"Yeah, Bert was proud to have had as many wives as Henry the eighth."

"He didn't give up easy."

"So, to avoid a similar fiasco, what do I say about you?"

"What's the rush? Do I look sick?" asked Chunker.

"You are a bit pale."

"No wonder. There hasn't been a stick of sun for months?"

"There are tanning places."

"They give you cancer."

"True but our health is reflected in our guises."

"Our what?"

"Guise, how we look. I read that in *Men's Health* at Dr. Willow's."

"You were at Dr. Willow's? Is there something he isn't telling me?"

"Like you should drop a few pounds?"

"I'm cutting back. I didn't ask for more fries."

"But you insisted we come to Eat Lots which keeps its promise of quantity rather than quality."

"Don't get off track. What besides Bert's ceremony is behind your talk about funeral speeches?"

"Who can predict when someone suddenly gets a fatal disease like Bert did? Then when death is hanging outside the door, everyone puts on earmuffs and pretends the patient will last forever."

"Well I'm in good health except for the few pounds, which Janet doesn't mind."

"What about accidents? I read yesterday that a cow fell through a roof unto a guy and killed him."

"*Coffee News* is not a reliable source of information. Besides when was the last time you saw a cow on a roof?"

"It could be a horse."

"We live in the center of town, how many horses do you see?"

"Did you know that if someone dropped a coin from the top of a skyscraper, and it hit you, you'd be a goner?"

"We have no skyscrapers, and if someone chucks a coin off city hall—proud at two stories—I'll take my chances."

"Or you could be murdered in cold blood."

"The only one who threatens to murder me is Janet when I forget to take out the garbage."

"Sure but now you're in the money you're a likely target."

"I hardly call the $5,000 I won at Bingo, money. Anyhow no one except you and Janet know and she's the only one who'd benefit. She couldn't risk it. They always look to the spouse first."

Mention of his wife reminded Chunker he'd promised to go straight home after the funeral to aerate the back yard although why Janet's sudden interest in the garden was a mystery. It wasn't as if they were selling the place.

Later that night noticing the tell tale ketchup mark on Bert's shirt, Janet said. "You've been eating fries? You want me to be widowed? The insurance doesn't kick in for another three months?"

Insurance? He'd forgotten about that. Janet and Fred had persuaded him to buy a policy pointing out that if Janet died (but why would she, she was healthy as a horse) he would be a rich man. But what if he died first?

"You know," his wife said. "Poor old Bert lived such a careful life and then died fairly young. We should live while we can. Do something daring. Well, you should, you're more athletic than I am. I'll cheer you on."

"Like dragon boating?" Chunker asked.

"No, you need water to do that, like bungee jumping. There's an intro course at the community center that promises you can be in top form in a few months."

Chunker slouched down on the couch, suddenly alert to the clues. He pictured Fred sauntering to the front of the church, and wading into his prepared speech. All the while planning how to sell the house with the well-aerated lawn. Before the deed was signed, he and Janet would take off to someplace exotic to spend his life insurance money. But how would they do it? Get him skydiving and cut the parachute line? He'd fool them and not do anything risky.

Janet squeezed in beside him on the sofa and pinched him awake. "I'm sorry to be such a nag. Why shouldn't you have a Huge Burger and fries? And as many beers as you like. Enjoy TV, forget exercise, it's boring. You only live once."

Gotcha, he thought, that is exactly what he would do. He'd live his once. From now on he'd only drink two or three beers a day even if Fred urged him to join him for a fourth. And he'd have no fries, well few fries. And he'd walk the block to the pub. He'd outlive Janet and

Fred and end up living the high life on his own insurance earnings and he'd only come back to town to speak at their funerals.

(Originally published: *The Dirty Pool*, 2018)

Downsizing

Having successfully changed the overhead light bulb, Jessica tentatively balanced on a collapsing packing box, and proudly surveyed her treasures clustered below. She had liberated her small hoard of favorite possessions from the garage. Would they, in turn, liberate her?

Changing the light bulb was child's play compared to her struggles over the last three weeks to realign her world to her satisfaction. She had taken her husband Terry's advice, though she doubted he would be happy with the choices she'd made, which was not surprising as they seldom agreed.

One thing they had agreed on was their need for some guidance in their downsizing exercise. The *Chaos to Control* workshop, hyped as it was, had been worth the effort. At considerable cost, she and Terry had ended up with a step-by-step how-to to go from a crammed garage, cupboards that belched angrily when opened, jam-packed drawers that hid necessities underneath never used items, to a clean sweep: everything divided as directed.

The manual was written in what was referred to as "accessible, practical steps to move from chaos to order." While Terry was in Ontario, seeking a job and affordable (cheap) accommodations, Jessica was left behind in Vancouver tasked with taking the downsizing and packing process from theory to practice.

Her husband, anxious about leaving Jessica to do the job, had decided to use his sweet side and leave on a high, hopefully effective, note. Before departing for the airport, he had sailed in the door with a pot of flowers in hand. She doubted that Terry remembered that the heavy scent of lilies made her think of funerals and took the high road. After all it was the thought that counted.

"Sit," her husband had commanded thrusting the flowers at her. He then pulled up a dining room chair opposite, taken her hands in his (as he had when they first dated) and smiled.

"Your friend Alice chided me for leaving you with so much work. She has a point." (Impressed by Alice's position as vice-president of a local moving company, Terry was inclined to listen to her advice.) "Getting rid of things is a lot for someone like you to take on."

"What do you mean, someone like me?"

"Don't be mulish. You know you don't like to throw things out, even things you don't need. And you attribute feelings even to inanimate object. Who else, over 6 years of age, would worry about chucking an old guitar?"

"It was my first one. I feel sorry for things that aren't appreciated."

"Very worthy, I'm sure, but now you have to be mature. Money's tight and the new place will be smaller. At first, we'll be spending time with my family so we won't need extra china and chairs. And a lot of what we have is junk. When I get the job I deserve, I don't expect to entertain the boss on an IKEA dining room table."

Jessica promised to be strong and follow the Downsizer's advise to the letter, at whatever cost. After she dropped Terry at the airport, she retreated to a local café. Her spirits buoyed by a cappuccino, she reviewed the manual, did some deep breathing and headed home for the face-off.

Following the professional Downsizer's advice, she divided Terry and her belongings into three categories: What you need to survive, what makes you happy and what just takes up space. Demoting things to that last category was a challenge.

Years earlier, Alice had christened Jessica The Hopeful Hoarder because she kept things such as her scuba gear that she hoped to use in happier times. But she'd also kept things—a broken rattan chair and tattered beaded jacket—she felt duty bound to repair.

Inspired by the Downsizer's speech, she'd relegated the "need some work" items to the taking up space category and dragged them off to the thrift shop.

Necessities had been delivered to her funky new apartment or shipped across the country. Now, scattered on the living room floor were things that Jessica had kept because they would make her happy: the green pup tent, downy sleeping bag and fold-up chair, ready for her first camping adventure in a decade; the scuba gear not needed on museum holidays; the leash waiting expectantly for a dog (Terry preferred cats); mystery books not learned enough for their library.

Soon, Terry, himself a victim of downsizing, would return from his foray east having instructed her to trim their possessions to the bone. "I'm not paying to drag your odds and ends across the country, so follow the Downsizer's criteria to a T." She had done as asked.

The phone rang. Jessica rushed to answer it. Leaping over the debris, she splattered on the freezer box, hopped across the room, and grasped the receiver in time to hear the message. "It's me. I'm in a taxi heading home a day early. Job secured. We can stay at Aunt Betty's short term. Heat some soup and open a bottle of bubbly. Time to celebrate."

Jessica sunk onto her camping stool. She had no speech prepared. Terry was better at responding to unwelcome announcements: quick, decisive, allowing no room for interjections. She wasn't as fast on her feet.

Her message would have said: Your furniture shipped to Ottawa, bachelor apartment rented here for me. All packed up: no pot for soup, and no glasses for champagne.

The key turned in the lock. A head poked around the corner, "Oh God," her husband groaned. "You got rid of the sofa to make room in the van for junk? I told you to follow the Downsizer's advice."

"I did," Jessica replied cheerfully, rubbing her swollen ankle. "As he instructed, I'm getting rid of something that I don't need to survive, takes up space and doesn't make me happy."

(Originally published: *Pilcrow and Dagger*, 2017)

Fish Eyes

To Alice's chagrin, fish eyes were the look for the upcoming year. And not just any fish eyes, mackerel eyes. Once again she would be out of step. She was stuck with her out-of-date cow eyes.

The desperate young girl leaned towards the mirror hoping to get a more encouraging view but, even in a subdued light, no wishful thinking could transform her large brown eyes into fish eyes.

She had searched the web for cosmetics or non-invasive surgery that would help. But even if she had the funds, Alice had been advised that neither would work. As the Make Over Guru had put it, what was needed for fish eyes were: round eyes dominated by large pupils (which could be created with drops but only worked for a few hours); both eyes situated close to the middle of the face; and no whites showing. It helped if your nose were flat.

"You're not having surgery for fish eyes," her aunt, the arbitrator of all things monetary, had said, "Next year it will be some other look, then what will you do?"

Unfortunately, Alice had been too young to benefit from the trend a few years earlier, when cow eyes were in vogue. At the time her teacher had scolded Alice's aunt for allowing her niece to look too mature for her age. When her aunt had protested that Alice had been born with those large limpid eyes the teacher had rolled her own cow eyes in envy, thinly veiled by disbelief.

Alice wondered if there was a country where fish eyes were not so popular. But she didn't know enough about geography to imagine where that would be. She assumed that now that everyone knew what was going on in every corner of the world, no country would ignore the trend.

And this year it was important that she look her best. She had her cow eyes fixed on a handsome prospect Jim Jack who was unimpressed with her knowledge of physics. The young man was an artist who insisted all science was suspect. "Beauty is my focus," he had said, "I only care for what is tomorrow." So although he didn't say it, Alice knew he was a fish eyes man.

"He sounds repellant," Alice's aunt had said. "I never trust artists. Look what they did with the canal. With all that plastic hanging over it and the purple water pumped in. It's no wonder there aren't any fish in there."

"Well Jim Jack didn't do that," Alice had insisted but the mention of the canal got her thinking. What had happened to all those fish? Of course their bodies had rotted but maybe their eyes had not disintegrated. If she could get hold of some eyeballs, she could dip them in plastic and stick them beside her own eyes, squeezed together to cover the rim of her nose.

Now that was a plan. For the first night in weeks, Alice went to sleep with sweet dreams. Wouldn't Jim Jack be surprised when she turned up at the summer dance, fish eyes gleaming?

The next morning, she announced to her aunt that she needed a net and some wading boots.

"Does this have something to do with fish eyes?" her aunt has asked. "If so I suggest you just feel proud to have aced your physics exam and wait until someone comes along who appreciates that."

"Tommy gave me a thumbs up when he heard I got the top mark," Alice admitted.

"So," her aunt replied. "Maybe he's a better bet."

Alice gave her aunt an evil stare and huffed off to her room. Humming along to the music on her earphones, she thought about how hard she had studied for that exam and how pumped she'd been with the result. But that didn't fix her eyes.

Tommy's hair stuck out in every direction but he was good at zoology. They were long time friends; maybe he could give her tips on how to create fish eyes.

(Originally published: *S/tick*, 2018)

Eye to Eye

"I haven't eaten a potato since I moved out." Such was the opening remark, after a winked hello, from Jennifer's new lover's soon- to-be ex-wife Brie.

The announcement, accompanied by a smug grin, flaunted Brie's anti-spud stand as a worthy accomplishment. This from the woman whom Jennifer had expected would outshine her at their first meeting?

On hearing the remark, Jennifer was annoyed that she'd allowed her insecurity to make the previous week a roller coaster of anxieties. When she and Barry could have been whirling through the bliss enjoyed by new lovers and walking the late night streets whispering intimacies, she had been preoccupied with the upcoming meeting. Her concern had been what, besides discussions about divvying up the spoils from a marriage gone wrong, she could talk about with Brie and Barry.

Her worst fear, as she lay stiffly beside Barry at two a.m. the day before Brie's visit, was that the subject of politics would arise and she would be left floundering.

Brie—a winner in everything but marriage—had an honors MA and was now working on her PhD. Besides being the editor of the Saxon University newspaper, she had run for office in a by-election and, representing a party that had to date never had its deposit returned, tripled the vote.

"You're as smart as she is," Barry had insisted. "And a much sweeter person. Brie is not very tolerant. She called me eccentric."

The word eccentric rang a bell with Jennifer. Her friend Bunty has used that word, albeit in an affectionate voice, when Barry ordered a side of potatoes with his spaghetti.

As to being eccentric, it was hardly conventional to come to your ex's apartment and, first thing off, announce to his new partner that you hadn't eaten a potato since you'd left. As if during their short marriage Barry had made Brie eat potatoes three meals a day.

Although Jennifer didn't consider Barry eccentric, she acknowledged that he was different: a one-of-a-kind old-fashioned guy. Unlike her previous boyfriend, Barry wasn't a macho man who spent more time in the gym than in her arms, never missed a chance to admire another woman's cleavage, and played war games on his I PAD as they watched her favourite TV show.

Jennifer was pleased with Barry. He was quite a catch. The only time they had ever disagreed, in the short while they had been together, had been on the question of Jennifer attending the meeting with Barry's ex Brie.

His insistence that she be there when Brie came to pick up her odds and ends had caused Jennifer a stressful week. When she had argued that she wasn't as interesting as Brie, Barry had said, "Everything about you is interesting. Potatoes are the only things as fascinating as you." She'd had a good laugh at that remark. Barry was such a wit.

Having reluctantly agreed to be present when Brie came over, Jennifer dithered about what she should wear, and whether she should offer beer or herbal tea. She had settled on wearing jeans and a T-shirt and decided to serve coffee and lemon cake. Thanks goodness she hadn't presented Brie with one of the six varieties of potato chips they had in stock.

Except for Brie's strange comment, the meeting had gone better than expected. When Jennifer opened the door, Brie had waltzed into the kitchen, plopped herself down and tossed out her potato remark.

After three weeks living with Barry, Jennifer knew her new romance preferred a traditional meal: meat, a vegetable and potatoes. Old fashion perhaps but hardly a problem.

But, as Barry noted, some people were narrow-minded. The week before, the waiter had scowled when Barry had asked for a side of fries with sushi. "Rice is nice," her sweetie had said, chucking her under the chin, "But 'tates are tastier."

The meeting with Barry and Brie had been short and sweet. Within an hour, Brie had carted off all the furniture and household goods she called her own, leaving behind a few wedding gifts, still in their boxes in the attic.

Jennifer had never heard of a woman who didn't bother to use or even appreciate her wedding presents. When she asked why, Brie had laughed scornfully. "That's another story. Final straw. They're all yours."

Jennifer concluded that, although Brie tried to appear happy that she was out of the relationship, the poor woman obviously was still in pain, which the sight of the gifts would have only worsened.

After Brie left, Barry and Jennifer settled onto two of the few remaining chairs and talked about how they'd keep their relationship strong. Jennifer suggested regular weekly dining out date-nights at which she imagined them sharing childhood secrets, dreams, and intimacies. As agreed, they did eat out weekly but candlelight suppers were peppered with conversation about the number of potato varieties, whether Peru was the potato capital of the world, the finest potato recipes from various continents, and ancient potato lore.

"The poor sweetie is so shy," she told Bunty. "Once he's more confident, we'll be whispering our innermost fears and aspirations, planning our future, our dream house, and when to start having kids.

When she moved in with Barry, Jennifer had brought all her worldly goods. To make room for her unpacked boxes, Barry suggested a storage space clean up. Jennifer agreed and took the opportunity to begin the process when Barry was checking his favorite potato sites on the Internet.

She decided to start with the hall cupboard under the stairs. She yanked open the stubborn door and a mountain of magazines cascaded out, knocking her down and covering all but her forehead.

After quickly saving a rare-find new potato website, Barry responded to her cry for help. As he pulled her from under the pile, he expressed concern about his scattered treasures. "Hope nothing got ripped," he said. "All of these are keepers. As are you," he laughed as an after-thought.

Jennifer was surprised to see such a range of potato related magazines, many in languages other than English. "Do you read Chinese?" she asked impressed by his skills.

"No but I enjoy the photos. Someday we can feature these in our potato archives."

"Do we have an archives"?"

"Not yet," he said with a wink.

Jennifer and Barry hoped to keep the romance alive by putting aside weekends as their special time to Be Together. One weekend they went to see a documentary on potatoes, another to visit a local potato farm where Barry volunteered and lovingly tended potatoes. One Saturday, the couple invited a potato expert to supper and heard about local farm practices. (Jennifer had had no idea so much of the local economy was based on tubers.)

While Jennifer was happy to spend time with Barry and to learn new things, after a few months she was ready to widen their range of activities. "Shall we try something new?" she'd suggested.

"Sure. Let's break out," Barry had said.

An hour later, he bustled into the kitchen waving the local newsletter, "It's opening this weekend," he cried.

"The show at the Art's Club?" Jennifer asked, pleased that patience had paid off.

"No, the farmer's market."

Jennifer had heard about the Market from a classmate. As well as organic fruit and vegetables there was local crafts, cappuccino and baked treats. Musicians were on hand to entertain and chefs, from high-end restaurants, explained how to prepare the more exotic vegetables.

"Good choice, I hear it's fun," Jennifer said, giving her sweetie a hug.

"Fantastic, they bring in potatoes from the valley: all sorts, mostly organic, all varieties, shapes and colors. I'm loyal to old potatoes strains, of course, but these new spring potatoes, properly seasoned, make a great side dish."

"Isn't there more than potatoes?"

"Could be. I never bother with anything else."

At least he's not interested in other women, Jennifer had thought but her confidence was shattered the day she came home early from school and heard Barry in the living room speaking in a tender whisper. "You are the dearest thing. Your skin like silk and your smell so sweet." She had thrown open the door to discover Barry fondling her rival: a small golden potato.

"Jennifer look at this darling spud," he said, "If only I could find a way to keep her young forever."

The longer they were together the more curious Jennifer got about the wedding presents. Barry's comment, "We can open that can of worms later," had set her wondering what was in those gift boxes that caused such bitterness?

One Sunday, when Barry was off at the organic farm, Jennifer ventured up to the attic. From the pale light seeping through the small triangular window she could see a pile of dusty boxes in the corner. It looked like they had been torn open and carelessly rewrapped. Jennifer carefully opened the first gift to discover one of four potato mashers (made in China). She then uncovered two potato ricers (one of German make), a set of eight potato tea towels (two from Ireland), sheets with hand embroidered potato plants, bathroom towels and a tablecloth featuring a spud motif, and more. Every item was related to potatoes. Jennifer concluded that Brie must have been over the moon in love to make a registry with a potato theme.

When Barry came home she fessed up immediately. "We've promised to be open with one another."

"Of course, " he said wiping the loam off his face. "Smell me, I am totally potato farm."

Not a pleasant odor, she thought but gave him a hug with her face to the side. "I peeked into the boxes with your wedding gifts."

"Good. Now we can enjoy them."

"Why is everything focused on potatoes?"

"Brie was in charge of the wedding registry."

"And only asked for potato related items? She must have been head over heals for you."

"On the contrary. When guests followed her registry, we ended up with a bunch of useless things: a blender, a toaster, a microwave, green bed sheets and other unnecessary items. Luckily, my brother Ted explained that wedding presents usually had gift certificates so you could go back to the store and exchange them. So I did. Every last one. Some of the things we might have used but we could get them second hand. Potato related items—like potatoes—are best if they're fresh from the box. And, in an emergency, if one masher breaks, it's good to have another on hand."

"Wasn't Brie angry?"

"Was she ever! She ranted and raved and even threw one masher out the window, which luckily was open. I put everything back in the boxes and stored them in the attic for safe keeping until Brie saw reason."

A month after Jennifer had set up in her new apartment she got a call from Barry. "I've met a new woman—well a girl actually—she wants to move in so I thought you should come by and pick up your stuff. She's anxious to meet you."

Jennifer was glad of the opportunity. She'd left so quickly she'd not taken all her belongings. Although she had no fear of meeting the new girlfriend—a bouncy young undergrad she'd seen sitting with Barry in the cafeteria eating a stack of fries—it felt strange to come up to the door of what she still felt was her place and knock.

The young women—her fair hair swept up and fastened in little potato clips—threw open the door and smiled broadly, "So glad to meet you. I heard good things about you, not from Barry of course, who is a little hard on his exes, but at the University.

Jennifer was guided into the kitchen to be greeted by a large plate of potato scones cooling and the unmistakable aroma of potato tea steeping."I haven't eaten a potato since I left," Jennifer blurted.

The remark was met with an indulgent smile from her replacement. "Barry said you weren't very tolerant."

(Originally published: *Romantic Ruckus*, 2014.)

And You Are?

Strolling down the street, swinging his umbrella and minding his own business, Richard pulled up abruptly on finding that a favorite pub, the Crab and Crow, had been razed to the ground. Where years earlier, he and his buddies had caroused, a commercial sign advertised soon-to-be-built condos and business opportunities. Good news that. Perhaps the local job prospects weren't as bad as he had feared.

He was jarred from his optimistic daydream when a hulk from behind plowed into him. The men faced one another, primed for a shouting match, but the attacker, with a jerk of the head, wacked Richard on the back and shouted. "It's you! For the love of God."

Stumbling to regain his balance, Richard scraped his memory to find a picture of the hefty man of about his age, decked out in low-slung mustard colored jogging pants. The guy was bouncing from leg to leg, a smile cracking to his ears. "You're looking good. Glad you're back on your feet."

This was the moment that Richard had dreaded when he and his wife Sara considered escaping to his hometown to live at his parent's old place.

"They may be off the beaten track but they read the papers," he'd said. "Those who haven't escaped town gloat when things turn out badly for those who have."

"Nonsense, charges were dropped. You overestimate your celebrity," his wife had snapped.

The stranger, seemingly aware of, but not put off by, Richard's recent notoriety, tossed back his black mane in delight. "I never expected to see you again alive."

"Alive?" Richard squeaked. Had the media suggested a disgruntled shareholder would bump him off?

"I wouldn't have missed your memorial."

Maybe this guy was an ambulance chaser whose only social activity was attending funerals thought Richard, relieved when the stranger continued, "However long it's been, I never miss an old pal's funeral. It's the one time the old gang surfaces."

Like crabs from under a stone, Richard—no sentimentalist—sighed.

"What you up to?" the stranger asked and, before Richard had time to reply, volunteered: "I was in the Middle East, but when my contract ran out we came back to the old homestead."

"Still active?" Richard asked, hoping to get a hint about who the guy was.

"Not like we were. Always up to something, eh? Remember the pig incident?"

He did not.

"More fun than the memory lapses of age," he should have said and admitted, with his roguish smile, that he didn't know the guy's name or the school or whatever. Instead, on glancing at his watch, he gasped as if horrified he was going to be late for an important appointment (not his actual destination: the dry cleaner), and muttered, "Great to see you. Crazy day, no time to chat."

"Let's get together. Talk about old times," the stranger said.

"Sure thing."

"We missed you at the reunion."

Richard couldn't remember hearing about a reunion but he would have avoided it had he been invited.

As Richard attempted to slip off, the stranger grabbed him by the arm.

"Whoa there buddy. Where do you live?"

Next thing he knew, Richard had given out his address and phone number.

Freed at last, he rushed home to tell Sara he'd been recognized, even with the glasses and stubble. She was one step ahead of him; someone had already rung their unlisted number. An hour later there was another call with a message that the caller would try again at suppertime.

Primed to lunge for phone calls from possible employers, Richard answered the third call briskly and succumbed when Mr. Unknown insisted on meeting for coffee with a flexibility of when and where impossible to sidestep.

All evening Richard and Sara kept returning to the question of the stranger's identity: Was he a forgotten acquaintance who considered himself a friend or was he a journalist hoping for a juicy story?

Next morning, when Richard arrived at the Eat-Here Diner, his 'old mate', was hidden in a back booth. "Small towns are hotbeds for gossip, which we don't want. Right!"

"Certainly not."

"You're probably wondering why I was so anxious to get together."

"Yes, I am," Richard confessed, waiting for the shoe to drop.

"I could use you."

"Use me?" Did the guy know he'd been exonerated of charges?

"Thought we could work together," the stranger said, causing Richard to wonder if the fellow had been in the Middle East when he was given the tarnished handshake.

"You don't have to take a high profile. I'll use your brains not your mug!" That followed by a volcanic laugh.

Over 55, near bankruptcy and worried he'd never get another job, Richard went for the stranger's offer. Sara was less eager.

"Who is he? Ask for his webpage?"

"It's apparently under his name, which I don't know."

"Insist on a contract. Check him up before you commit."

"He's drafting something which I'm to sign when we meet for lunch."

"Hasn't he got an office?"

"Yes on Main Street but it's being renovated."

The next morning, for the first time in months, Richard woke eager to face the day. He checked his e-mail to find the promised job description, and there it was: short and sweet. He hadn't done marketing since he moved up the ladder but he'd catch on quickly.

Once again at their Diner table, the stranger said, "I'll have office space for you unless you prefer to work at home."

"No, an office sounds great," Richard said, pleased at the opportunity to get out from under Sara's nose. He took the proffered contract, flipped over the front page and read the small print. All seemed okay.

"Check your address and put in your social insurance number," his boss-to-be said.

Richard glanced at the front page: Contractor Tom Higgins. The name didn't ring a bell. Obviously the recent stress had put a strain on his memory or this was an early "senior's moment." Never mind, at least his employer now had a name. With a sigh, Richard moved to the final line. Consultant: Hudson Clarke. Who the hell was that?

(Originally published: *InfectiveNK*, 2016)

Aspirations

The moment the crown was placed on her head Matilda acknowledged that even the acclaim that came with winning the regional Pickle Eating Contest—second year in a row—was as naught. Matilda's passion was sheep; her goal was to be a shepherdess.

She had joined the swaying group of people who were successes in the world's eyes but who were in their own, more discerning estimations, failures. Matilda had known of these people for years: whenever she saw stories about them she'd get out the scissors. She had a scrapbook ready to receive the clippings.

But that day it had been revealed to her that her mission was to write a book outlining their frustrations. Who better? Her personal experience would be the final chapter. She'd call it: "Joining the Successes." Celebrities like Sibelius who had written tunes so catchy that even she recognized them to Sullivan, of Gilbert and Sullivan, who wrote those upbeat melodies but wanted to compose symphonies.

Even as a toddler Matilda only liked stories like Noah's Ark and Jesus' birth. (She had been certain there had been sheep modestly hiding at the back of the manger.) As for nursery rhymes Mary and her little lamb had been a favorite, although Matilda had insisted that Mary's lamb would have preferred to wander the hills rather than go to school. "Even if he were academically inclined how can even a little lamb fit comfortably in such tiny seats?"

Over the years, she had tried every avenue to reach her shepherdess' goal. To succeed, she required sheep and to this end had consulted the owner of the local feed store about lambs in the area. "More a cattle district," Bobbin had said, staring out the window at the open range.

When Matilda advertised her aspirations on-line she discovered that local shepherdess' opportunities were limited. "Send me a photo, I'd like a little shepherding," said one cocky responder who was immediately filed in the trash.

Not easily discouraged, the image of herself with her little herd moving across the hills persisted. Under a bright night sky, they'd hunker down as she—staff in hand—kept a sharp eye out for wolves. But here again Matilda was thwarted; the local park ranger insisted that there were no wolves for two hundred miles. And what wolf would go that far for supper?

So the day after the Pickle award, Matilda, with help from her librarian friend, put together a query letter linking her experience to the others to be featured in the book she planned to write: "As one who shares their angst, I can describe the pain of aspirants (14 examples) who ended up celebrated among the many, but frustrated professionally," she wrote.

Satisfied, she was on the right track at last, that night, as Matilda drifted off to sleep, counting sheep, she speculated whether the book cover should have a photo of her in her Pickle crown or a line drawing of her on a hillside, in a bonnet, with her beloved sheep.

(Originally published: *The Short Humour Site*, 2003)

Beating the Odds

The Eureka moment when Ron Ronaldson discovered how to live to 113 was quickly followed by drag-in-the-dirt hours agonizing over how to handle his discovery.

Should he divorce his wife? He had promised to love Moira "till death do us part" but that was when he expected that they'd die at approximately the same time. Now he had discovered how to live another 58 years, but his wife, who never followed his advice, would likely die within the next thirty. Much as he loved Moira, he wondered if he should divorce her when he still had a chance at another long-term relationship.

The monetary possibilities also concerned him. Should he make a quick buck or take the high road and share his discovery freely. In the past, when he shared his insights with his drinking buddies, they scoffed. However, if he didn't impart his new found wisdom and his pals dropped like flies, when he reached 110 he'd be laughing in his beer at a table for one.

It was the day of Jimmy's funeral that Ron's discovery hit him like a bolt of lightening (albeit not as painfully). He'd wrangled the afternoon off from his part-time pizza delivery job on the pretext that Jimmy was a high school buddy. As the funeral music faded, Ron had slipped out the church door and high tailed it to the pub.

It was there, perusing a week-old newspaper that Ron read that if you stopped smoking you would live longer. Jimmy had been a smoker and a heavy one at that so it was no wonder he was pushing up daisies. (Actually, Jimmy had been cremated but same idea.)

Then Ron remembered reading the week before that if you ate less of some kind of fat you would live longer. When he put two and two together, he was on a roll. After supper (perhaps the last time he would eat such a life-sucking meal) Ron sequestered himself in his den. There, sipping his coffee (still to be determined if this was a year cutter), he perused the pile of newspapers stacked in the corner waiting for him to clip significant articles.

Often the research was fuzzy. It started out bravely suggesting that years could be added to your life if you did such and such but as the story progressed there seemed to be a lot of ifs and buts. Ron regretted he hadn't done his math homework in high school. Statistics weren't his strong point. Still, from what he had read, Ron figured that each plus should be worth at least a year. Even on his first run through, he had built up a good number of easily achievable years.

(Being of a scientific bent, Ron ignored things that didn't apply. For example, he read that aardvarks did not get leprosy but he couldn't see how that would help most Canadians so he ignored that data. Apparently, Andorra had the highest life expectancy at 83.5 but Ron didn't know where that was so he couldn't in all honesty recommend moving there.)

From a personal point of view, many of the dos and don'ts didn't seem difficult. He got a few years for being a Caucasian male. (Being a woman would have improved the odds but he held the line at a sex change.) He lived in British Columbia so that gave him the highest life expectancy in Canada and in a city, which was better than rural life for years earned. Owning a pet gave you a boost and cats were easy to come by. Moderate drinkers lived longer so a heavy drinker like himself should be even better off. Churchgoers lived longer and he had been to church just the day before at the funeral. Married folks lived longer and he had chalked up 30 years on that front.

As Moira, who knew nothing of good health, would attest he was a complainer and research proved complainers lived longer. Six or seven hour's sleep gave you an advantage and on weekends—given half a chance—he slept 'til noon. Those with a healthy sex life lived longer so he would cut out the late night horror movies and join his wife in a tumble. His discovery had put him over the moon, which was win-win as being happy gave you bonus years.

It was past midnight when Ron finished clipping and sorting. He planned to get up early the next morning and head for the library. The young librarian was a whiz at finding information on the Internet. He wanted to ensure his information was reliable and the more he knew, the better, but even with this initial research, he was pumped.

Why hadn't someone else caught onto this? Forget the fountain of youth; it was just a case of following his checklist. He would call it Ron Ronaldson's *Live Forever Diet.* Well, no that was exaggerating, not forever, and he'd avoid the word diet, which was worn thin. Thin? A pun, maybe he could use that in his speech. "This is not a diet it is a *die not yet.*"

Fame was in the cards. Just like the guy who was bonked with an apple and discovered gravity (and nowadays who scoffed at that?), he'd made a scientific breakthrough. And this was a very important one; he'd discovered how to live at least thirty years longer.

There was a book in this, for sure. Of course, a magazine article would be quicker but you probably didn't make much from magazines. More importantly, unless you wrote a book you didn't go on speaking tours and they brought in large crowds who in turn would buy your books and videos. He could see the billboard already, "Ron Ronaldson speaking tonight on How to Live to 113. Limited seats available."

Would $75 be too much to charge? He would certainly have to get folks to keep his formula secret or the dollars would bleed away.

That evening, glancing in the mirror as he washed his teeth (good dental care, surely a few months for that) Ron considered whether he should get a hairpiece. Recently the camera flash made him look slightly bald, that wouldn't look good on his book cover or promotional materials.

Raising his upper lip to study his reflection, Ron considered getting his front teeth straightened. Of course, as a celebrity he'd count on soft lighting and professional makeup like T.V. broadcasters used, to help his image. Luckily, all these improvements could be chalked up to business expenses but he needed a sharp accountant and soon. His mind was still spinning as he hit the pillow.

The next morning, when his wife passed him his plate of bacon and eggs Ron winked and said, "Not for me, love. I'll take soy sausages if you have them."

"Soy what?" she said. "What do think I'm running: a health food store?"

Ron vetoed the coffee, checked the label on the orange juice, and finally informed his wife that he had to head to the office.

"What office?" she asked.

"I'll be using the public library for my office until I get set up."

Moira popped on her glasses to check his outfit. "Why've got your good jacket on? Has someone else died?"

"No, I can't look too casual in case someone takes photos."

"Since when?"

"Since my first day as an upcoming celebrity," Ron said soaring out the door.

"Celebrity at what?" his wife shouted. "Have you got another wife and family somewhere?"

"No way," he called back. "I'm sticking with you. I'm not like one of those lottery winners who drop their wife at the first million." (He was ashamed he'd even considered leaving Moira, she was a grand old girl.)

"You've won the lottery?" his wife cried, leaping up and spattering her Yummy-Os across the counter. "We're rich."

"No, I didn't win the lottery," he shot back. "But as good as."

"Is this about Jimmy's death," she called after him and caught his cry "Right on," as he ducked around the corner not slowing down to explain.

On that happiest day of his life, Ron skipped down the street, swinging his umbrella and, as Mrs. Burton later informed the reporters, clipping her gladiolas. Twirling through the possibilities, he burst unto Main Street failing to notice the No. 7 bus swing round the corner.

The report on page three of the local paper noted that had he not risked his life by jaywalking, Ron might have lived for another thirty years.

(Originally published: *Writers Tribe Review*, 2013.)

Jeremy Irons

"Jeremy Irons," a voice squealed.

I looked up to see a woman, a few years younger than me, face aglow, her long black coat flapping open, gripping a tenuously burdened tray.

"Mind if I join you?" she said indicating that the other tables at the small diner were all occupied.

What could I say? Unable to read anything but headlines due to my bleary eyes, I was having a breather before heading back to the office to argue budgets with my boss. At my reluctant nod the woman sunk down and laid out her food, leaving barely room for my coffee cup.

"Of course you're not Jeremy," she admitted cheerfully. "What would he be doing in a pokey café like this? But you're sure a ringer."

I fumbled for the newspaper to hide my pleasure at the comment. No one had ever suggested I looked like a celebrity.

"Do you get asked that often?" she continued.

"No."

When my wife Angie and I first dated, she described me as having a teddy bear look. For some reason, she considered that attractive. Now with a few surplus pounds—kindly hidden that day by my coat—and a tendency to wear favorite sweaters long past the best-before date as Angie puts it, she is less complimentary. "You need to trim a few inches off your gut," she advises when I head for seconds. Or "Spend the money you waste on lottery tickets to replace that ratty sweater."

Not discouraged by my newspaper, my inquisitor thrust out her hand,

"Janice Wilkins."

"Mark Thomson," I replied with a reluctant shake.

"You know Jeremy though?" she said.

"Not personally," I said trying for a roguish look, which nowadays is seldom called upon. Attractive women, and Janice was that, never ask to share a table with me nor do they strike up a conversation.

"But I know his work," I added remembering him as an English actor who played rich upper class types who lived in stately homes.

"Very sexy," my tablemate said.

Noting the library book I'd picked up for Angie, Janice commented, "I usually read at lunch too but I just got drops in my eyes so I can hardly see."

"Me to," I confessed. We ended up talking about movies and books. "You're really well informed," she gushed.

Then just as we were well into a *My Dinner with Andre* scenario, Janice jumped up, "I have to get back to work. But this is my local watering hole so I'm sure we'll meet again."

Nice thought. Once I left the café I checked my *I Pad* for information on my look alike. Even on the small screen Jeremy looked a handsome, distinguished fellow, something that until then I hadn't considered myself. I would more aptly be described as average—that is average for a middle aged, middle class white man: brownish hair, five foot ten, not too fat, no distinguishing marks (excepting that crocodile tattoo I found on my left ankle the morning after my 41st birthday stag).

I noted at once that Jeremy dressed well—debonair—and the effect set me thinking that I should buy some new clothes. Instead of plodding back to the office, I headed for the nearest department store.

Urged on by an effusive young clerk, "That's perfect for you," I bought two sweaters, a jacket ("so trimming") and a pair of slacks "You look ten years younger."

I felt in my prime when I sailed into the house. Even before taking my coat off, I proudly informed Angie, "A woman told me I looked like Jeremy Irons."

"You've got to be kidding."

"First glance she thought I *was* Jeremy Irons."

"Was she short sighted?"

That evening I headed to Video Classics—the last video store standing—and got a VCR starring my double. On first view of Jeremy, I felt the bond, here I was finally connected with my—what did the Germans call it my twin—doppelsomething.

I was grateful that Dr.Grimsby had advised me to switch to contact lenses. My old glasses (one arm poorly mended) made me look like an unfashionable old fogey.

When I had noted in the store mirror that my posture was not as erect as was Jeremy's, I resolved to stand tall, and subsequently checked my stance in shop windows as I passed by. My improvements were noted.

"Are you up to something?" Angie queried, catching me in front of the bedroom mirror admiring my new look.

"What do you mean?"

"According to *Women and Wear*, a man who suddenly pays attention to his appearance is probably having an affair."

I laughed but then, a few days later, our neighbor—a comely widow—gave me a wink, "Mark you're looking great."

But although I was obviously putting a spark in women's eyes and my double Jeremy surely had affairs, I'd no intention of straying.

Two weeks later, a changed man, having been fitted for my contacts and sporting a new jacket, I spotted Janice sitting at "our" table. There were empty seats but I made bold to ask, "Mind if I share?"

"Please do, Jeremy," she winked and displayed the book she'd been reading, "Your recommendation. First-class but challenging."

What could I say? Jeremy and I are intellectuals.

"I apologize for last time," Janice said. "You were too polite to say I was crazy."

Distinguished and polite, that was Jeremy and I all over.

"Apologize for what?"

"I'm a glitz with names. You look nothing like Jeremy Irons. It was Jack Black I meant. You know that scruffy, loveable guy who looks like a teddy bear. "

(Originally published: *Halfway Down the Stairs*, 2013)

Do or Die

Flowers in hand, phone set to pulsate at regular intervals to remind him to appear attentive, and a cheat sheet of appropriate responses Leonard was ready to follow the tips about a romantic dinner he'd read about in his men's magazine. Gloria was worth the effort, and according to her ultimatum, this was a do or die occasion.

A week ago, sailing into their fifth anniversary, his wife had declared the romance had been squeezed out of their relationship, which she had described as a kitchen rag only useful for cleaning the counter. Where, Leonard wondered, did she dredge up these images?

Gloria had found an article in a women's blog advising that when things hit bottom a romantic dinner was in order. "We'll go to Pavlova's restaurant and talk about life," she said. "And with the cell phones turned off."

Whoops, Leonard had thought. That was an expensive restaurant. There goes three months of lottery tickets. And what was there to say about life? Wisely, although Gloria insisted he share his thoughts, Leonard decided not to share these.

Both dressed in their Sunday best, his pants a bit tight and her dress somewhat revealing, they were tucked into a corner table at Pavlova's.

"We'll pretend we're lovers on a first date."

"Sure," he obliged, thinking a quick hand squeeze might work well here.

He remembered how on an early date, chomping down on Gloria's great BBQ ribs, he'd noticed the handyman work that needed doing in her apartment. While in the bathroom, he'd tried to fix the dripping toilet tank and cracked the lid. Gloria had responded to his apology with a dizzying smile.

But now that their toilet at home needed fixing she was less cheerful.

"I want us to share the spiritual experience of being outdoors," Gloria said leaning across the table.

If they bought a new toilet, they could get one that used less water.

"And to travel" she said.

He glanced down at his cheat sheet. "Just what I've been thinking."

Did those toilets cost more? More importantly did they get rid of number two?

"Sailing on the Danube."

Where was the Danube anyhow? He'd thought it was just the name of some highbrow music.

"If we want kids we have to decide soon," she sighed.

His phone vibrated and he glanced at his cheat sheet. "Those were my thoughts," he said.

If new toilets were expensive, he'd get his friend Joe Rump to fix the old one.

"You look worried," Gloria said. "What are you thinking?"

He squinted to read, "How you look prettier than when I met you."

It was funny that his plumber friend was named Rump.

From success to success—appear attentive, read a line, smile—the evening was a triumph. As they toasted their anniversary over coffee, Gloria flashed one of her chrome bumper smiles. "Let's head home to get this baby plan in place."

Baby plan? Had his missed something? If they had kids they'd need a second bathroom. Instead of sharing that thought, Leonard just pecked his wife's cheek and used up his last line. I'm so we had our talk.

(Originally published: *The Short Humour Site*, 2012)

The Fine Print

Being of sound mind, I never believe ads. And although I never read the fine print, I always tick off 'agreed'. As a result, I am now confined to a basement room watching foreign feet pass by the window.

Recently, having reached the age when I couldn't count on many more decades of life, I was desperate to enjoy a few more kicks at the can. Meager as my finances were, I was determined to see the capitals of Europe and one night, spurred on by a large rum and coke, I decided to search, if necessary 'til dawn, for a real deal. And then like a mirage on the desert, it appeared.

"See Rome and die," the ad beckoned backed by a stunning photo of the eternal city and an unbelievable low price. I had to put my glasses on and off a few times, to be sure I wasn't mistaken but no, there it was. The price, which was half the normal fare, included a stay at a hotel and city tours.

I had always promised myself to see Red Square before I died—and in the winter at that—but the Russian leader had dampened my spirits. But Rome: the eternal city, the home of Romulus et al. Yes, yes, I would do it.

Mesmerized by the video I pictured myself escorted around town on the tour bus, imbibing in a glass of wine at a small café, laughing and skipping along ancient winding alleys with the group.

Nervously checking my credit limit, I was delighted to discover that assuming I could live off what was in my larder for a few weeks and kept my credit card in my pocket, I could make it.

Yes, yes. All-inclusive: flight to Rome, small friendly tour, central hotel and all meals. Wow, wonderful. 'Only three spaces left' blasted across the screen and seven minutes to commit.

Carpe diem. All systems go. With shaking fingers I filled in the form. I quickly scrolled to the end of the fine print and clicked off 'agreed.'

One minute flashed on the screen. I would just make it. Adrenaline pumped through my veins like good wine down my gullet. And success, I did it. I printed out the receipt and collapsed back. Hats off to me. For once I took a chance, bit the bullet, seized the moment. It was all I could do to stop myself from bursting into the street and crowing.

The next morning, when I bragged to my sister about my upcoming holiday, she made a prune mouth and said there had to be a catch. Rome was probably so crowded with gangs of mafia they had to entice people to go there.

Two weeks into the tour, some of the happiest hours of my life under my belt I was gloating about how wrong my sister had been. There had been no catch. Later that afternoon, the tour guide took me aside, and whispered in my ear. Being a bit hard of hearing—and no chance of affording hearing aids this year—when I asked him to speak louder he said.

"You didn't fill in part two of the fine print so we need to discuss it now. Tomorrow is the last day."

"But I ticked 'agreed' and paid."

"There was a glitch; it should never have let you come without filling out the last page. Heads will roll."

"Not mine," I laughed, my mood being considerably lightened by two weeks in the eternal city.

"Not unless you choose that. Unusual but it's your choice."

"Choice of what?"

"How you want to die."

"Oh," I chuckled, "You mean I can choose as my last night: indulgence in chocolate or wine for my way out. Not like that Pope who died with a surfeit of lampreys. Of course he really did die." I added enjoying the attention of the guide—a rather good-looking guy who to date had focused on younger patrons.

"As you are?"

"Pardon"

"Going to die, but you have a choice how. We can't do the lions in the coliseum as the humane society has banned that. Otherwise its all systems go."

"But not really dying."

"Oh yes. The ad was clear for the amount you paid it was see Rome and die. Otherwise it would have cost twice the fare."

My adrenaline pumped, my heart started to swell like a helium balloon and my brain raced around looking for some way out. "But that was just an ad," I sputtered.

"All legal," my guide smiled. "Your choice."

"I need to go to my embassy, " I spurted. "To address a last minute issue."

"Of course," the guide said patting my hand encouragingly.

Five hours later I was holed up in the Embassy. The travel company had someone stationed out front. " Just to be sure you don't skip town," the guide said.

"We won't kick you out," a staff member said, "On taking the deal, you chose suicide but it's illegal in our country so you are stuck here unless something can be worked out."

"At least you're in Rome," my sister e-mailed. "It's an adventure."

What kind of an adventure is it watching feet shuffle down the road from a basement window? Even the prospect of a million dollar story with the *National Enquirer* for my survivors is little comfort.

(Originally published: *Dodging the Rain*, 2018.)

A Shipboard Romance

Betsy's suddenly found her two romantic fantasies—remarrying one's first love and a shipboard romance—unexpectedly within reach.

As a teenager, Betsy had read about the remarriage of Richard Burton, what a voice, and Elizabeth Taylor, what a face, and longed to imitate such passion. Her husband Peter was out of the running for remarriage as they weren't divorced and his only passions were his work and betting on the horses.

But the possibility of a shipboard romance had materialized when her sister, having come into money, offered Betsy a weeklong cruise and a promise to look after the home front. However, as always with her sibling, there had been a catch.

"You have to promise that on the cruise you won't mention how your workaholic husband drives you crazy."

"Okay, will do."

"And not drone on about the girls: the tooth aches, ballet recitals, etc."

"Why all the rules?"

"You have a chance to be free and kick up your heals. Sitting in a corner, like you do at parties, waxing eloquent about how cute Trixie is in her new dress or how stubborn Lucy is about homework won't make you friends."

"I have friends."

"I mean shipboard friends."

And, for once, her sister was right. At dinner, on the cruise no one talked about kids or errant spouses, instead they told of the exotic destinations they had visited or the day's excursion. Betsy relished the tales of adventures and imagined possibilities for future trips. One man, Thomas, a gentleman with no wife in tow, became her dance partner on the dress-up nights and a companion on deck surveying the stars.

Betsy realized she'd done it: a shipboard romance. When they arrived back in port, Thomas slipped her his card, asked for her e-mail (no harm in that) and stood with her on the deck (like on the Titanic but drier) as they docked. She had planned to take the bus home, having assured her sister that she had no need to pick her up.

But suddenly to her horror, there on the quay, waving like crazy, were her five girls decked out in straw hats, polka dot blue dresses and smiles. Her sister, standing behind them, gave her a shrug and a grin.

Betsy jumped when a voice behind said, "Look at that adorable group of girls: probably a school group. I'm sorry and I Rita didn't have kids. I'd sweep those ones up in a jiffy. Then I'd never worry how to spend the weekend and finally have an excuse to go to the fall fair.

Wow, Betsy thought. Dreams come true. Now if she could only sidetrack her husband with an agreement to remarry again later, she could enjoy the best of both worlds.

(Originally published: *The Short Humour Site*, 2019

The Dudes in the Dell

On finally digesting the transforming word "gig" over the din of the pub noise, the friends sailed above the deflating grumbles of wives and bosses into a sunny future. Only on considering task number 7, did they detect the sound of a their hot air balloon hissing. Before that expectations were high…

"We've got a gig," Trevor had crowed, rushing through the crowd to his pals in the corner booth. When his friends, crunched into their regular table didn't cheer at the good news, Trevor waved a wad of paper and roared, "A gig. Here's the contract."

"A gig?" said Bert.

"An event, an engagement, our chance to shine," screeched Trevor.

"I know what a gig is but are we ready?"

"If you wait until you're ready you'll never sail," said Elmer.

"When's the gig?" Mark said, checking his day timer to see the event didn't conflict with his dental appointment.

"Two weeks from today. The other group—Dickson's Dreadnaughts'—drummer dropped out when his wife left. So we're in."

"Two weeks? Our suits might not be adjusted by then," warned Elmer, the designated outfitter.

Bert, ever cautious, held up a hand. "Whoa Bessie, let's get the details."

"It's for the Easy Eat celebration at the mess hall. We play from 8 to 1 a.m."

"That's late," said Elmer. "By the time we put our gear away and get home, it'll be close to 2. "

"That's show business," Mark noted wisely.

"Which is what we're in now," Trevor cried, "Show biz."

Although, they all felt pumped, they were determined to show what Bert called "due restraint."

Now, they were heading for the big time, they had to proceed carefully. They'd often discussed the risk of groups of having one big hit and fading because of lack of planning.

For years, the girls—or as Mark's wife insisted they be called women—had met twice a month for a book club meeting. They touted it as a chance to get together and talk about more than sports.

The men also met bi-monthly. "To drink, " as Bert's wife said. "We talk too," he'd argued. "About sports and things."

Four months earlier, the guys, after a number of beers, decided they would do something to impress the ladies. Not only their ladies but birds in general, and they came up with the idea of forming a band.

"Ladies love musicians," Trevor had assured them.

They decided not to tell their wives until they had their first gig, knowing the women would douse their plans with negative comments such as: "So now you're great musicians." or "You guys never follow through."

True, in the past, the friends had lost steam the morning after pub night but they vowed that this time their wives would be proven wrong. Much time had been spent discussing the look on the ladies' faces when they were taken to the first gig. And that moment was near.

"Another round on me," Mark offered heading for the bar. "It's time to celebrate."

"Yeah but we need to get organized," said worrywart Bert rummaging through his briefcase. He pulled out the To Do list written in marker on a large sheet of foolscap. Although graced with beer-can rings and faded ketchup marks, the list was still legible.

"We have almost everything in place," said Trevor.

"Yes," noted Elmer adjusting his glasses to admire the check marks. "We got the gig, which was 2nd last on the list."

"Okay but we have to be sure our ducks are lined up," said Bert.

To date the group's biggest challenge had been picking a name. There were only four of them, all over 50 and none too svelte, so the first suggestion—The Boys in the Band—was vetoed.

"It's not really a band," Bert had said, more of a group. "Boys in the Group."

And we're not exactly boys," noted Mark. "Some of the hot shots today are in their teens."

Armed with another pint of the cheapest if not the best, the men read down the list from 1 to 7. Getting the gig had been challenging so it had been put near the bottom with the most difficult task relegated to number 7.

It had been Mark who noted, "The motivational guy said to start with small, achievable items."

"So from the top," Trevor called out, his marker in hand to add a tick to the check mark.

1. Commit to the Concept. (Another idea from Mark's workshop.) Tick.

2. Choose a name. Three months in the process they'd finally decided on: "The Dudes in the Dell." (The Dell outside town was just a lurch in the land, but who was to know.) Tick.

3. Decide on the type of music. (They'd agreed to follow demand. "More jobs that way," said Bert. "Whatever: popular, jazz.") Tick.

4. Identify places and events to play at. (Lots of ideas." Celebrations." "Wherever we're wanted that pays." "Churches, arenas." "We can do weddings or divorces.") Tick.

5. Get Dramatic Stage Outfits. (Success on-line, inexpensive, red velvety two pieces suits. "They can be adjusted to fit," Elmer assured them. "And sequins look great on stage.") Tick.

6. Get gigs. (Not as hard as they'd expected.) Tick.

"We only got two weeks," said forever wary Bert "We'd better get to number 7."

7. Choose and learn to play instruments.

(Originally published: *Intrinsick,* 2015)

Barry Pope-Pope

"So how was I to be chosen Pope?" Barry prompted, pouring Mindy more green tea to entice her to continue.

"I don't know," she shrugged, "You know they lock them in a room to vote."

"Who they?"

Barry was eager to know details about his nomination for Pope, or as she put it Pope-Pope, but as usual once Mindy had regaled him with her dream, she lost interest.

"Who are they?" he prodded.

"Bishops or something, I don't know I'm not a bloody Catholic."

"Neither am I which is why it's funny you'd dream I was Pope."

"It was because of that TV show last night about how rich the Popes were. What a good life they had: all the servants and posh palaces."

"Better still, all the booze and good food."

"That too, I thought you'd enjoy it: sitting around pontificating."

"Better still sitting around eating and drinking, but back to the hitch that I'm not Catholic."

"You'd be the first Zoroaster to be Pope."

"Maybe not. Wasn't there one who took Jerusalem?

"But that was for the other side."

"The dark side?"

"Whatever," she said, "Which is why you had to be Pope-Pope."

"But did you see me in Pope's robes?"

She stirred her tea, glanced at her watch and shrugged, "Sure, they had a dress rehearsal to see how you'd look. You were in your gear: gold and purple and red velvet."

"And I looked good?"

"Yeah, you looked great. And you had on that little hat, so you couldn't notice your hair."

"What do you mean, Notice my hair?"

"That it's not thick."

"Are you're saying I'm going bald?"

Mindy rolled her eyes, "Focus on the positive," she warned.

She was right. Until now, Mindy had complained that his job at Billy's Best was a dead end (ignoring the fact that he supervised the students) and threatened to find "a better catch." The dream showed that subconsciously Mindy could see him doing great things; maybe being on a TV reality show or a CEO of some company.

Unless he had jumped to the wrong conclusion, maybe being Pope was a bad sign, "I thought you hated the Pope," he said.

"I hate the real Pope because he won't let Catholics use birth control even in Africa with all those people dying of AIDS but you were a good Pope. And let me tell you getting it off with a Pope is hot."

That night in bed, mind buzzing, Barry wondered where he could rent a Pope costume. In a pinch, even a Bishop's robe might get Mindy going. But it might be a lost cause; they probably burned old robes or made them into cushion covers to keep them from non-believers like him.

Next morning, as Barry watched the student stocking the shelves his mind kept snapping back to himself as Pope-Pope. Mindy and he arm-in-arm, or maybe she'd be a respectful step behind. Other times, he'd be high above the crowd on the balcony waving or walking through the street touching babies' heads. The Security guards would try to keep him away from the crowds but he'd refuse to be separated from his people. And every night, he and Mindy would be going at it like rabbits in one of those high gold canopy beds.

"What's up, doc?" his co-worker Jennifer said when she caught him in the lunch room, mesmerized by his meatloaf sandwich.

"Just thinking," he smiled.

"It's probably about a raise or a week in Hawaii," she laughed.

"Or my life as Pope" he almost blurted before snapping his mouth shut in case she was Catholic.

At the bar after work when he told Fred about Mindy's dream his friend spurt out his beer, "You fucker you aren't even a Catholic and you sure ain't a celibate."

"A what?"

"A celibate you fucker, you sleep with women."

"Yeah, so."

"So you can't be Pope besides not being Italian and not even being a Catholic."

"It was a dream, stupid, but it shows what Mindy thinks of me."

"She thinks you're religious?"

"No, that I am Pope material," he said, finally recognizing that Mindy's description of Fred as 'always thinking inside the box' was right on.

The more Barry considered what the dream meant, the more powerful it made him feel. It was obvious what an impressive figure he was in Mindy's eyes. His stride strengthened and he stood proud as he glided along the aisles past the frozen food. Sure he might have preferred if she had dreamed he was a superhero but the Pope was still a very important guy.

As soon as Barry got home, he began to badger Mindy for more details: Was he a shoe in? What would he do as Pope-Pope? Were lots of women after him? Which celebrities had he met?

She played along for a while making up details about meeting movie stars and sleeping on satin sheets, but finally exasperated that he was interrupting her favourite TV show, she sputtered, "Oh for Christ's sakes, it was just a dream."

"But it shows that subconsciously you see me as Pope or President or something."

"Piss off. I made it up for a laugh."

"No way."

"Yeah way, it was a joke."

His bones suddenly chilled cold as a dip in a May lake, his stomach collapsed as the long robes slipped off his shoulders.

"But you said you dreamt it."

"You're so incredulous."

"Don't you mean credulous?"

"Always nit picking, counting cans."

"But that's my job."

"Which is why you'll never be Pope."

(Originally published: *Speech Bubble,* 2011)

www.ingramcontent.com/pod-product-compliance
Lightning Source LLC
Chambersburg PA
CBHW022158160726
48282CB00024B/241
9789388319324